(PCT) Psychological Counseling Therapies PLLC

GOOD MENTAL HEALTH WITH DR. MIKE
(A DUAL-DIAGNOSIS TREATMENT APPROACH TO MENTAL HEALTH AND SUBSTANCE USE ISSUES)

MICHAEL A. GRAY, EDD, LP

(A compilation of Dr. Gray's work and other resources that he uses for Dual-Diagnosis programming in the PCT practice.)

Table of Contents

INTRODUCTION-
A New Approach to Treatment

I have found that as I work in the mental health field in various capacities, there are therapists with limited life experiences which does not equip them to provide needed treatment for clients. (Or, their educational pursuits are not fully developed to allow for the best treatment environment possible). Invariably, the therapist may rely on textbook approaches which are heavy on emotional attention without a practical, results oriented approach. A practical, results oriented approach would allow the client to develop elevated self-esteem that which comes from success in treatment (and success in life). Elevated self-esteem sets the stage for more successes and this piggybacks into improvements that should be the focus of treatment.

A second problem set of issues affecting treatment is that the client enters treatment with dysfunctional thinking (on a general level), thus, they do not implement the changes from treatment effectively. For these reasons, (as well as other reasons), I provide this introduction to cover necessary points and concerns associated with setting the table for long-term, success in treatment. These are just some of the issues to be addressed to allow the client to benefit optimally from their treatment experience.

A popular model for describing depression (also having applications for other mental health issues such as anxiety or substance use) is that one first has (1) a trigger (or triggers) that activate the symptomology associated with the disorder. Then (2), the person ruminates over those symptoms (a preoccupation during the day and racing mind at night when they try to unwind to sleep). Lastly, and finally, (3) the person avoids the actions necessary to correct the issues that caused the problem symptoms. Things continue to spiral downward thus client sinks deeper into their depression. Many therapists want the client to address how the problem makes them "feel". This is nothing more than ruminating as best I can tell when considered from a practical manner. Clients need relief from the issues, not to consider the feelings associated with feeling bad. My question remains, why does one wish to dig the hole deeper? (Continuing to feel the depression is nothing short of rumination, is it not?. In short, with many therapists the client is stuck in step 2).

When the client enters treatment, I must address some functional issues with their basic thinking and expression to set the stage for success that propels the client forward. Since the thinking of the client may often be the proximal cause for their disorders, the thinking must be attacked and amended. **First, the client must**

consider that everything that they say they also hear. When they say that they "can't" or "but" to others they are also telling themselves that they can't. (Or, I think you are right, "but" is their way to deny change). I deny their continued reliance in those ways of describing their life in their discussions with me and ask them to avoid this thinking going forward categorically. What is the likelihood that the will change their life when they tell others (and themselves) that they "can't" do something? I am not foolish enough to believe that believing in self is a guarantee for success-however, they vastly improve their chances for growth by avoiding the expression of (and subsequent decision-making based on) that thinking.

We don't always have to "do" or "make" something happen. This is nothing more than a plan to "control" their life circumstances. We truly have control over very little and must exercise "faith" to help us continue to demonstrate "hope" for that future. **The serenity prayer suggests that we must exercise "acceptance" and "allow" life to unfold**. I encourage my clients to do their best but, then, allow the future to work out the kinks. A truism remains that most of what we have worried about never happened. We must exercise faith and patience and the therapist must always remind the client that they are in a marathon called life, not a fifty-yard sprint called today.

An initial issue that the addict, or the mentally dysfunction-related concerned demonstrates, is the idea that their problems or challenges give them license to be noncompliant or unproductive. I have continually heard from those who are early in treatment express excuses for no shows for appointments or failure to complete goals because of …… (fill in the blank). (Remember- "can't never did anything" (my father's words to me as a small youth). **Everyone has problems to deal with; the difference between achieving a sense of personal mastery (or not) is that one deals with life-not making the problems justification for failure or inactivity.**

One of the first things that many of my clients must do is take care of ensuring themselves as financially viable-from this initial necessity most future successes occur. **When a person is not employed they still have a job. Their job is to get a job.** Since they would expect to work 8 hours or more generally, they must actively apply for employment the same number of hours (or more) every day of the typical work week. If they do, I have not typically seen them look for over 2 weeks to find work. You must put the time in to gain the desired result. This is a basic start point for the addict when they begin the process of changing their lifestyle. Since it is near impossible to work and maintain a drug habit, work takes the place of (and precedent over) drug use when actively engaged in recovery.

Stop describing their life based on how they feel. Make their understanding of their life based on reason with deductive-logic oriented thinking that results in behaviors that get things done- not just to satisfy their emotional comfort. Our feelings will bring us pleasure for a season but there will always be a payday. This is a basic spiritual reality that supports the notion that emotions as a basis for behavior lead to a destructive end (when not managed by rational thought). Further, the client must redirect their expression when it centers on the negativity of their life perspective. When they express a negative self-assessment of their situation, they must immediately qualify the comments with any positive aspects associated with the subject under discussion. Things that are slanted tend to go toward the overloaded direction so don't let the negativity become the status quo.

Self-esteem is not improved by feeling good, rather, self-esteem is elevated by experiencing success from achieving goals (rather than mere words). Properly assessed, the treatment process is a laboratory to help the client develop good life skills that promote success which, in turn, leads to experienced success in both treatment and life. (This is the reason why some of my core areas in this manual are there). This is the only consistently effective way to "feel" better (gaining resources thru effort).

Physical health and mental health are not mutually exclusive of the other. Often, I have seen patients who were irritable and angry, depressed, or anxious because they felt bad physically. The core area in the manual-emotionally self-regulating behaviors- is included for this reason. Exercise is one of the least prescribed yet most effective ways to improve mood and functioning. Structure daily regarding sleep, diet, exercise, leisure, and spiritual practices are essential.

Many individuals have mental health issues because of a dysfunctional approach to their interpersonal relationships. Yes, you love and hope for the best for those in your life (or) expect others to behave appropriately but, **the only person you have any actual control over is yourself. The only person responsible for your happiness is yourself.** The likelihood that all, or many, of those in your interpersonal circle will live up to your rules is slim to none. There are always issues in the lives of others (in spite of our wishful thinking). **If your mental health is dependent on another's happiness (or others acting appropriately), you will be angry, depressed, bitter, or anxious as a rule-more often than not.**

When the therapist works with clients in individual (or group) therapy, they are also conducting family therapy. The changes that the individual makes affect the structure of the family unit and the family members must also adjust to the new reality of a changed client. In the manual the developmental models are discussed to not only help clients to gain insight as to how they got to their present place. I want them to understand how they can ensure that their children (and other family members) can avoid similar pitfalls that the client has experienced.

We need to break the cycle of addiction and other problematic mental health issues when we can.

I have consistently been told by my clients that they have been in therapy for, in many instances, many years. **They share with me that they feel they are in beneficial therapy for the first time when they see me and attend my groups.** The consensus is that the typical treatment environment centers on discussing triggers, urges, how they "feel", and their drug history and use. They leave these previous therapy experiences with the "urge to just go out and use because drugs are all we talked about". Also, there is typically a lack of a cohesive "plan" for treatment with well-established goals and strategies to be met. (I know that everyone wants to think that they are "special" but, truth is that there are many typical reoccurring themes for the addict or mental health issues being treated).

My treatment objectives are different. I want the addict to experience changes for the better in their situation (a job, apartment, car, paid fines, etc.) so that they (as they report to me over-and-over again), "I am happy with my life now and don't want to go back to using again". "Things are just so much better now- why would I want to ruin that?" That is infinitely more important than hammering away at limited substance abuse treatment terms (triggers and urges) that could be effectively covered in a brief treatment as part of a larger therapy designed to provide tools to deal with mental health issues as the manual accomplishes.

The learning, for the client, is predicated on the client taking personal ownership of the materials in this manual. A person can memorize information only to forget it unless they take their learning experience to a deeper level. This is accomplished by application of the materials and concepts to their own lives so that the information becomes their own. The terms, categories, concepts, etc. within this manual, when applied to the client's individual situation become a part of their functioning. This help to form a lifestyle better equipping them to live productively. **I want the client to be able to identify behavioral techniques and thinking categories (as examples of things that I anticipate the client will master) but also why it is such. That shows me that they have conceptualized the materials into their everyday existence.**

I hope that you benefit from this manual and find that it, when studied in its entirety, fits together as a puzzle with each piece bringing the tools and perspectives needed to effectively change the lifestyle of the person. This occurs by using this manual. Be aware, cherry picking the materials and not viewing the manual in its entirety is not helpful as the total manual must be considered to gain the overall goals to this approach to therapy. Knowledge is both power and liberty- study it to gain these things. This is the true test of effective treatment- stopping using a substance or correcting a mental health symptom is the short-term goal. **Identifying problems is the first step to correction through personal awareness.**

Changing the person for the better (with a new lifestyle) is what is the true test of effective mental health treatment. There must be an actual plan-for both treatment as well as one devised and implemented by the client to realize their desires. **(Without a plan one will aimlessly go thru life usually only reacting- rather than being proactive).** Having a plan keeps treatment beneficial and, for the client, it is essential to have a plan to measure success and keep the client on point to grow and change to a better place. Make the goals "specific" and "measurable" is important. Being there for the client for the potholes while making them take personal responsibility for implementing those goal is the therapist role. Success breeds success, and, success will increase the self-efficacy (feelings about one's abilities on a certain thing) of the client to continue to explore their plan for living.

Finally, I do not promote a religion (that's a personal thing)-rather, I encourage every client to have a personal relationship with whatever they believe their Creator to be. The amount of support that this relationship offers to the individual cannot be overlooked. In some instances, when things appear to be at their lowest point, this relationship may often be the thing that helps them hang on. Forget the humanistic ideal of only "living for the moment"- **make a plan for your life**, monitor your progress towards achieving those goals associated with the plan, change the plan when necessary, continue to plan and expand your aim, and enjoy both your plans and your successes.

Be at peace with yourself, do not be a harsh taskmaster to self, dream big, and do not be the one who gets in the way of realizing both your ambitions and dreams. **Believe in both your Source, and yourself.**

CORE AREA ONE
Cognitive-Behavioral Therapy (CBT)- Dealing with Dysfunctional Lifestyles Using Rational Thinking (Step 1)

Why and how we do what we do- A look over the past 50+ years that has got us to where we are now.

The Origins of Cognitive Behavioral Therapy

Secular society gives credit to Aaron Beck for the beginning of CBT as a therapy model for helping people to deal with life.

Fact is that scripture has stated over 3,000 years ago (Proverbs) that, "So a man thinketh' in his heart, so is he". This clearly and plainly states the premise for CBT.

The premise behind CBT is that we (1) have a thought, then (2) have an emotional response to our thought, which ends with (3) a behavior.

My experience is that modern society often places more emphasis on feeling good (emotion) than being good (behavior based on thinking) which is at the cause for most of our present problems.

Rules of Modern Society- The crux of the problem

What is apparent to this writer is that society has developed certain rules for life that are problematic for the best mental health of our citizens, among these rules are;

1. **One must be happy and, if not happy, then one must take actions to be happy.**

2. **If one is not happy just take a pill-then one will be happy.** (Having "things" to be happy is another avenue to travel for some).

3. **If it is legal, then it must be OK.** (Do you agree with what is codified as socially permissible?).

4. **Live for the moment because we may not have tomorrow.** (Preference for instant gratification- this is a humanistic concept that has proven to derail social interest in long-term commitment).

5. **If it is out of sight then it is out of mind, or, if it does not stop me from getting my needs met then don't worry about it.** (Failure to consider that things they do not address socially will affect others important to them-either now or their off-springs).

The Change Concerning Happiness

I overheard as a lad in the early 1960's on a repeated basis from older high school and adult individuals that they "don't take poison into their bodies" (When drugs were offered to them by a few of their peers).

At this time with the advent of advertising on media the big advertisers included slogans such as "making life better through chemistry" (example- DuPont chemicals). This ad campaign was followed up by (approximately 5 to 7 years later) slogans such as "making life better through medicine for your health". (This was after aspirin became a household fixture).

Since people were (and are) bombarded by television and radio with sales pitches we have become affected by marketing and accepted their claims as facts as "they must be telling the truth because I heard it on TV".

NOTE* (Another "rule")- **6. TV and those on television "do not lie").** Reality is that marketing is designed to serve the one paying for the ad and sell their product as the primary purpose (or so it theoretically seems safe to consider- not for the consumer's interest primarily).

It appears that the conceptual change regarding happiness is that, in the past 4 decades coming up to the present, happiness is gained by something happening-not having the person striving to be happy in spite of what does, or does not, occur. Such a goal requires the person to find happiness from within- rather than from their environment and our culture's distractions ensure the looking from without self rather within self.

An Assessment of "Progress" Over the Past to Present in Thinking

With this advent of the "miracle" drug and of medication as a fix for problems relating to medical and mental health issues- we have seen the United States be primarily moderated by substances ingestion to address those issues. We make up a minor fraction of the overall world population but make up over 90% of the consumption of anti-depressants. The figures for other psychopharmacological drugs is similar in percentages. (Our social expectation is generally that we address <u>not</u> feeling good-physically or mentally- with a substance, thus, our reliance on drugs and medications to a potential fault).

With the advent of the automobile and its availability for the general population after WWII, the family became mobile which led to relocations away from the previous close daily contact of neighboring family members of multiple generations. (Often for employment promotions, careers, weather, or health). Besides not having the guidance readily available from senior generations for the adolescent family member, media took on the role (to a greater degree) of providing information. **(The concept (for many) that better finances will buy more and better things which, in turn, promote happiness).**

The explosion of aids and inventions to make daily life easier with less time necessary to address basic needs. This has resulted in more free time. This time, for many, is taken up with distractions such as entertainment and substances to "feel good". This also parallels a drastic alteration to lifestyles wherein traditional, spiritual and religious attendance has plummeted.

The end result being that there appears to be a society that depends on feelings based on secular concepts to an ever-increasing degree such as materialism and hedonism. This, in turn, results in the behaviors and sociological trends described above (if one is to examine the actual results of our new-found changes).

Note that this change is not systemic of all, just that an ever-increasing number reflects this as each succeeding generation comes into our cultural civilization. For many, lives are managed and preoccupied by gadgets.

Examining the Rules?

When do we get the most learning from an experience? Is it when we experience success, or, is it when we fail?

Is not failure a growth experience?

Is it even realistic to be happy all the time-what mindset realistically believes that we will be happy all of the time?

Taking pills or doing drugs are ways of distracting one's self away from reality or it seems appropriate to consider. (Be aware that many things function as a form of distraction away from self-reflection). Further truth is that most distractions do keep us away from addressing our own selves.

Only ask yourself about a variety of social issues that have been given legal sanction- Are they OK with you?

Happiness-A goal or a journey?

When your child was born, or you graduated from school or a training program, or you had time with your family at a family event did you experience happiness?

Can drugs or medications compare with their effects on the same level of happiness as any of these mentioned events?

The question concerning the "rule" about happiness is this; **Are drugs, medications, or alcohol a source of happiness or, is it a distraction** (alteration to the brain's functioning in reality) **to avoid dealing with whatever is actually wrong and determining (and implementing) change for growth and personal improvements?**

NOTE* THIS IS THE PRIMARY GOAL OF THIS MANUAL- TO ENCOURAGE SELF EXAMINATION BASED ON PERSONAL REFLECTION TO IMPROVE FUNCTIONING.

Freudian Principle Regarding Human Functioning

The Freudian concept of the balancing of the **pleasure principle versus the reality principle** is what is at concern in most instances as-

People are trying to find a pleasurable state while avoiding pain and anxiety (Pleasure Principle). On the other hand, People will not do some things because they will be arrested, injured, embarrassed, or shunned and humiliated by others (Reality Principle).

The key is that we need to be balanced much the same way as a see-saw with neither the pleasure principle nor the reality principle out-weighing the other. When balance does not occur, there will be either distress from over indulgence (drugs, sex, and/or alcohol) or the basis for a rigid personality from being overly judgmental and mean-spirited.

Balance and moderation are the keys.

The Dichotomy between Objective Reality versus Subjective Reality

There is a difference between fact and opinion which is another way of saying that there is a difference between thinking and feeling.

Thinking has traditionally been associated with facts, data, and rational/analytical reasoning. It has been associated with reaching "truth".

Emotional reasoning does not require facts or data-one merely "feels" a certain way and there is no accountability for their feelings. They "just are".

Thinking and rational facts do not provide anyone a preference or privilege as all are equally obligated to abide by these facts.

Feelings, on the other hand, are based on who is in power as to what is considered OK- there is no equal and level playing field for all to operate from.

STEP ONE – THE THOUGHT

In order to function effectively one must start with a rational thought. This is the first step to the CBT method.

Aaron Beck suggested that there are, at minimum, 13 categories of bad thinking known as "irrational thinking" (otherwise known as Dysfunctional Thoughts).

These dysfunctional thought categories are at the beginning factor for most of the problems that cause conflict, depression, anxiety, substance abuse, etc.

Without appropriate or effective thinking processes there is no need to examine the two subsequent steps (Emotions and Behaviors).

13 CATEGORIES OF IRRATIONAL/DYSFUNCTIONAL THINKING (Beck)

#1- All-or-Nothing Thinking

This is at the core of compulsions and obsessions as one goes from one extreme to the other extreme rather than being grounded in a balanced, centered lifestyle. Extremes in behavior are also consistent with a bipolar presentation.
This is a feature of a concrete, rigid personality that is very set in one's ways without the benefit of being flexible and able to deal with challenges. (They see things in a literal way without understanding hidden meanings. As a result they end up with anxiety, depression, or anger. The irrational nature to this category is that there are seldom instances when this idea is accurate-there are usually always exceptions and varying points on the spectrum rather than on either end only.

#2- Jumping to Conclusions

Besides being a source of antagonism for others when you don't give them time to explain or expound on a thought, is an obvious dysfunctional type of thinking.

What is suggested is that we can complete others sentences or thoughts and that we don't respect others enough to allow them to converse with us.

A major and obvious result is that we tend to be overbearing and hard to approach to share time with others when we disallow them the time to process what they are thinking with us.

#3- Fortune Telling

Statements that start with "I bet you" or "I see" or "I know" are sure fire examples of one's attempts to fortune tell what is in store for others or what others are going to do or experience. Since much of the communication that we are engaged in is an attempt to make decisions or to consider options it is counter-productive to short circuit others by a quick "I bet you" statement when we really do not know what is or can happen without some doubt.

#4- Focusing on the Negative

This tendency is predominate for those who operate from a depressed or bipolar (depressed end to spectrum) state. The have a tendency to approach everything from a negative way and rarely are the source of any positive, happy communications.

These people frequently find themselves alone as most do not want to invest a great deal of time with them-people prefer positive and happy people.

#5- Disqualifying the Positive

The common test regarding people is "Do they see the glass as half full or half empty". Those who fail to find a positive "rainbow" at the end of the storm are those who focus on the negative by ignoring the good things that are part of the situation.

It is easier to find common ground with others when one is able to overcome the problems and focus on the things that are both good and bringing people together in situations rather than those things which separate people.

There is usually some "good" in practically any situation if we look hard enough-it is a real gift to be able to see it.

#6- Allness or Neverness

I often hear people say when they experience rejection or failure that "this is the way it always is for me" or "I never have anything turn out right".

Another common statement is that "I never have anything good happen". OH REALLY? If a person has "never" had anything turn out right then it would be too improbable to believe. The challenge to this thinking is to be able to effectively "weigh" the "good" and the "bad". The mental health dysfunction that comes from this is a depressed and anxious state because we anticipate the bad so that even if the experience was 75% good- they would focus on the 25% bad portion.

#7- Minimizing

This is a way of invalidating the positive as not having any importance while allowing the bad in a circumstance to be what is that which is remembered. There is a general lack of gratitude when we fail to appreciate the good and give thanks. A follow up to this is that credit needs to be given to whomever or whatever was responsible for our blessing(s). It is very important to give appropriate weight to things to fully appreciate or realize the importance to them. Failure to do so places us in a position of a future disaster that we have not adequately prepared for.

#8- Emotional Reasoning

I have only rarely found that emotions lead to long-term positive experiences. The scriptural adage that "there is pleasure in sin for a season" suggests that at some future point the results would outweigh the benefit of engaging in the activity. This adage is important in considering the danger of engaging in emotional reasoning. Common results include criminal activities, obligations that we are not prepared to take on, or the full range of mental health issues such as anxiety, depression, addiction, and dysfunctional personality styles.

#9- Labeling & Generalizing

This is common behavior that is associated with discrimination and prejudice. No matter what race, ethnic, nationality, gender, or age there are difference in all of us. When we stereotypically consider these categories we fail to respect and appreciate the differences in us all that make us special. It is imperative that we realize as a part of our spiritual development to grow in our appreciation for our fellow human beings.
Never is it accurate to state that "everyone does that" or "everyone knows that" or that "everyone- anything". It is just not true. This is the way that one suggests to other people that their way of behaving or thinking is the "right way" by saying "everyone" does what they believe or think.

#10- Personalizing

Common practice is to suggest that when someone does something that is a problem for another – they did that to "me".
People do thing to "get their needs met" so it is not done because of anyone else in more cases than not. People do not consistently do things because they "have

it in for me" as is suggested by those who depend on personalizing others thoughts, feelings, and behaviors.

Personalizing others actions allows the personizing behavior to avoid considering the reasoning and genius behind others actions. They had a reason for doing what they did-we need to consider their reasons as a growth experience rather than an affront to oneself.

#11- Phonyism

This is rather clear as we can all see instances when others are not genuine in their treatment of us and others. The spiritual rule that must be considered is "Do we do thing for others with the end result being that our needs end up being met as a byproduct of placing others first- OR- is it all about us without caring or taking others into account above us"? A truth is that once the phony behavior is realized the person will experience rejection and become isolated because others will avoid them. This is a source of mental health dysfunction. Another way of viewing this is to ask whether the idealized expressions of what one says they believe in and value are actually practiced in their daily lives- not doing so is phony in practice.

#12- Perfectionism

Regarding mental health issues- this is at the core of OCD as a predominate symptom for the disorder. The anxiety that results when this dysfunctional thinking process is not met leads to a host of interpersonal issues and substance abusing behaviors.

The world is not perfect and perfection is not attainable. This is a reality that is ignored by those who have a need to have control over their environment.

Since we cannot control the sun rising or setting, the seasons of the year, the earth or the planets, or have a certainty to our time on the planet we-in reality, do not have control. The illogical nature of perfectionism ignores these truths.

#13- Mustabation

This category makes girls blush and men giggle. However, it is at the core of most of the problems in our interpersonal world.

The definition of "mustabation" is that we believe that "things must, should, or ought to be a certain way". This is totally illogical to believe as people do not operate based on what we believe they should do, ought to do, or must do.

When they don't behave as we wish or expect-What do we do? We are angry, irritated, distressed, depressed, anxious, or other detrimental emotional states. This is self-evident to be at the core of mental health issues. This is beyond any doubt I suppose.

BEYOND THE CATEGORIES-CONSIDERING OUR THINKING

There are two basic ways that a thought occurs-

(1) The thought occurs with ourselves – In this instance we need consider the categories so that we don't duplicate a category of thinking that is dysfunctional.

(2) The thought is shared with others – in this instance (after being self-assured of the accuracy or appropriateness of the thought) the communication model is used to have an interpersonal experience.

The simplest Communication Model is – the Sender, the Message, and the Receiver. This goes back and forth between the one conveying the thought and the one receiving the thought, and vice versa.

Possible Outcomes from the Expressed Thought

We can either- agree, disagree, don't understand, need more information, ignore, or don't care. These are the general ways we can approach the thought. Often, we are busy thinking or considering what we will say in response rather than hearing and considering what all the other person(s) have or are saying.
There is one other option that is frequently initiated by the receiver of the message by altering, amending, or outright ignoring the message by, in effect, **"taking the message somewhere".** It goes something like this;

"TAKING IT SOMEWHERE" .... (A Source of Dysfunction and Mental Illness)

While the suitor is talking to the object of his interest, she is "taking it somewhere", (in her mind) such as- "Does he think I am pretty?, Does he like me?, Is he smart?, will he make a good father?, will he love me?, can I trust him?, will he be a good provider?, will he respect me?, am I stupid, ugly, or fat?"
Meanwhile, He is "taking it somewhere" as he is trying to figure out how to win the object of his efforts.
They may invariably end the exchange as sad, nervous, depressed, anxious, or happy- all emotional experiences that are largely absent a primary concern for a rational-based assessment of their possible relationship based upon considering what was actually said by, and to, each person.

The Problem with "Taking it Somewhere"

The need to communicate without respecting each other enough to hear, in totality, what the other is saying is at the start of much misunderstanding and conflict.

If we are unwilling or unable to allow each other to fully express their concerns, we lose out on a possible positive experience. We limit our options and possibilities due to turning others off and missing out on potential friendships and beneficial business opportunities.

We may also plant the seeds for Mental Health Problems. QUESTION- (If one "takes it somewhere" every minute, of every hour, of every day, of every month, and for a number of years, why would one not expect to have mental health problems?) ASSESSING OUR THINKING- "Metacognitive" Functioning

Metacognition is defined as "thinking about thinking". (See Worksheet 1 **(WK 1)** at back of the book to practice this concept).

We need to spend time daily doing this as a meditative practice. If we are able to determine that we are falling into the traps of the categories of irrational/dysfunctional thinking and, further, that we avoid taking other's conversations and thought somewhere-we still must take our self- awareness to another level.

We must do a thought check that examines the origins of our thoughts and whether they are good, appropriate, and effective for us. CBT (Beck) theorized that our thinking's origins and functions are on three levels to determine their value.

How Does this Meditative Method Work? (Consider our thinking and reflect on it from the most obvious to the deepest level to ascertain the accuracy to our thinking- start wit the first level and work back to the third (deepest level)-it the 1st and 2nd level are not supported by the 3rd level then we need to leave the thoughts alone as being primarily poor choices.

Three Levels of the Thought (or Belief)

1st level- The blurted-out expression when we become aware of something such as "oh, darn, oh, damn, etc." This blurted out expression was the outward expression of a privately held belief or thought that is the basis for how we try to behave or is the basis for what we believe.

2nd level- the privately held belief or thought. This is a learned thought that has been devised as an interpretation of our world and our interactions within it. Even though we should be constantly evaluating these rules or beliefs for their appropriateness most people just stick to them without much reflection or alterations. This is a problem.

The deepest, **(3rd) level** of the thought, is the schema or foundation rules that one typically learns as a child or in school. These are the basis of social functioning such as the 10 Commandments or the "Golden Rule".

Self-Monitoring as a Way to Deal with Dysfunction and Mental Health

When you were a child you were told to sit in the back of the car and be quiet until you arrived at your destination. Asking "are we there yet" was not well received. You were expected to just look out the window and be quiet.

As an adult you are expected to communicate with your Significant Other in order to have a good relationship. During the trip, each person's input is essential. This is in opposition to the earlier time.

Point being, life is about change and what was once a good way to think or behave is not necessary most effective in the future. Asking oneself about the 3 levels of thought-are they true, are they beneficial, or are they appropriate on an ongoing basis, is necessary to avoid problems.

Common Statement by Those Who Enter Treatment for SA/MH Issues

In practically every instance that I listen to the new client who comes in for services is the statement that "I wasn't thinking" or "I felt................" (An emotion- instead of thinking).

The common theme is one of allowing emotional living to override common sense and good judgment. Common sense and good judgment are arrived at by thinking and the thinking is in a manner that is effective-not dysfunctional.

A primary way to help people is to develop a problem-solving strategy (in Core Area 5) to assist them in dealing with issues in a consistent and effective manner. There are 4 ways to approach a problem or issue- You can ignore, avoid, deny, or deal with the problem or issue. Only dealing with it will ultimately work for your best interest.

Roadblocks to Thinking by the Person

"I don't know"- this common when someone does not want to take serious, significant effort to determine what the issues are, OR, they don't have much positive self-esteem regarding their abilities to determine what is wrong.

"can't" OR **"but"** – the first one is a way of denying themselves the opportunity to succeed by giving up (again also possible to be low self-esteem- how can they raise the self-esteem if they don't overcome their sense of incompetence?) OR "even though what you are saying is right or correct I will choose to do it my way"

(if their way hasn't worked thus far- "How is this time different if the same solution is attempted?")

(1- A)

CORE AREA ONE – DISCUSSION QUESTIONS

Four of the most important periodic self-review questions we must ask ourselves. (Your answers may cultivate self-awareness).

1- Am I happy? (why, or why not)

2- What is the problem? (be specific and measurable)

3- What do I want? (not only what you need)

4- Are my needs being met? (how so, or how not)

Situational questions to ask yourself. (These will help you make well-reasoned decisions.)

a. – DO YOU THINK BASED ON "FEELING GOOD", OR, ARE YOU MORE CONCERNED ABOUT THINKING OF WAYS TO "GET ER DONE"?

b.- ARE YOU PRIMARILY WORRIED ABOUT THE HERE AND NOW, OR, IS YOUR PLAN BASED ON THINKING FOR LONG RANGE GOAL(S) SATISFACTION?

c.- DO YOU BELIEVE THAT YOUR THOUGHTS ARE RATIONAL? (OR, ARE THEY JUST HELPING YOU TO GET YOUR NEEDS MET?)

d.- ARE YOUR THOUGHTS DEPRESSED, ANXIOUS, ANGRY, WORRIED, ETC? (DOES THIS WAY OF APPROACHING THINKING SEEM EFFECTIVE?)

e.- IF YOU KEEP DOING THE SAME THINGS WITHOUT CHANGING WHY WOULD YOU EXPECT A CHANGE IN YOUR CIRCUMSTANCES, OR, WHEN THINGS ARE NOT WORKING OUT WHY KEEEP DOING THE SAME THINGS OVER? (IN ADDICTION LITERATURE, THIS IS THE DEFINITION OF INSANITY).

REVIEW QUESTIONS ABOUT THE THINKING CORE AREA MATERIALS- (SKILLS BUILDING)

1. Identify the categories of dysfunctional thinking that you have used and give examples.

2. Identify a situation where metacognition would be helpful.

3. Discuss the concept of objective versus subjective realities- give examples to show that you have mastered the concepts.

4. Discuss times when you "take it somewhere" and how it has given you "facts" about yourself- AND are those "facts" actually objective reality or opinions?

5. Were you thinking or feeling when you experienced failure, rejection, errors in judgment, etc.?

CORE AREA TWO
EMOTIONS (CBT-Step 2)
The Modern-Day Preference by a Secular Society & the Onset of SA/MH Issues-

Emotions and the DSM (handbook of mental health disorders)

It is my estimation that close to, or, approximately 70% of the text of the manual which identifies mental health issues (entitled) Diagnostic Classifications for Mental Disorders (DSM) is either emotional-related (directly or indirectly tied to emotional behaviors or actions). In short, the modern-day clinician is, often times, treating emotions rather than the thinking or behaving of the client.

Emotions often have no rational basis thus they are difficult to be addressed by logic or analytical thought. Since they have few logical rules or basis-there is no fool-proof strategy to address them as people are different. You may be lucky and be able to hit on the issues or you may not do so. (Kinda' of like being in a dark room and trying to find the light switch).

It appears more effective to attempt to avoid the use and reliance on emotions when possible to maximize the potential resolution of mental health issues that require the client to seek out treatment. (By both the clinician and the client).

A simplified way of asking the obvious is in the following way. If you don't have an apple tree can you have apples? (Don't say I can go to the store and buy them-you know what the question is, I am sure.) So, if you don't rely on your emotions or acknowledge them as important to your life-they are less likely to take space in your head seems safe to assume in more situations than not.

The Ice cream sundae approach to emotional expression

If one has an ice cream sundae every day is it special? If they have once every week is it more special? And, if one has an ice cream sundae once a month is not indeed very special? The point is that reliance on emotions is most effective when it is done on par with the ice cream sundae strategy just mentioned.

Also, understand that we are emotional creatures and sometimes that is all we have. When we experience great loss or failure we may not have any other way to manage ourselves to make it through the moment except for experiencing and expressing emotions. However, beyond making it to a point when reason takes over, emotions should be a release of stress and tension-not serve as the basis for, or preferred means of reaching, solutions to the problem. (A spiritual adage is that we are allowed to "be angry, but do not act on it. Point is the adage can use any emotion for the subject- the predicate to the sentence remains "not act on it").

Why is emotion extremely common as a solution to problems?

For the longest time I could not understand why emotions were the most used means of dealing with life by my clients. Further, when looking at society and the multiple instances of societal dysfunction-emotions were usually used to establish social norms. As we look at the results of these social norms we find we all face on-going, severe problems resulting from poor planning based on emotions (typically absent reason).

Roughly 30%+ of the population has a college education-this equips them for knowledge for a small body of knowledge. Others have education for a trade or skill-this too is a small body of knowledge. Many spend their time with the media rather than reading (often times). Thus, most people have a limited knowledge base to work with. All they have left in many situations to deal with life is their emotions. This is a civilized society problem that is critically destructive to our best interest as a world, but many operate from emotions.

Loss of traditional knowledge sources = emotional dependence

Prior to the automobile, the family spent multiple generations in close residence to each other thus knowledge was passed down over multiple generations to the youngest generation. This equipping the youths with knowledge of a practical nature.

Prior to the demand and emphasis on college and media for knowledge, the scriptures were studied as a source of knowledge. Thus, they were equipping with a like or similar basis of understanding to allow for finding common ground. Since the older members of the family were readily available the potential for seasoned, well-developed solutions and thinking was present (and frequently) modeled for the youngest members.

Now, with increasing lack of parental (or role modeled) direction (due to parental absence from the household, priority for distractions over commitment, and working out of the house, etc.) stability from reasoned practical life skills is often absent. In the past, this was traditionally responsible for ensuring that established norms and traditions were passed down yet now this pattern has been altered. This leads to a lack of a consensus in perspective and a split between peoples beyond previous levels. Now opinions based on emotional reasoning is a more frequent norm and has become an alternative to rational, reasoned behaviors.

Consider the ineffectiveness of emotions for decision making

When one feels (emotion) stressed they may turn to cigarettes and drugs or alcohol as a way to "feel better". (Doing so to be accepted is just another way of feeling good by being "cool" or part of the crowd). How does this turn out 30 years later when you are told by your provider to get your paperwork together because you have cancer and there is no treatment for it? Or, when you become addicted to drugs and alcohol how effective was the decision to allow your emotions to serve as the basis for your decision? (Feeling good rather than facing life on its terms).

What happens when you find someone and you "fall in love" with them and procreate only to find, after spending some time with them, that you had made a big mistake? How effective was allowing emotions to serve as the basis for your decision? And, many pay.

Point is that I can go on with many examples when emotions led to a real problem with the lesson being that is more appropriate to rely on rational, critical-thinking rather than emotions and how you "feel".

Managing the Damage from Emotional Reasoning (STEP 1)

The most important question to ask when faced with our emotions that result from the thoughts we experience is- **WHY DO I FEEL THE WAY I DO [rather than] WHAT AM I FEELING?** By doing this simple step we take the situation away from the emotional context and return it to the 1st step which is that of "THINKING" rather than 2nd step of "EMOTION". This is the point when we examine our 3 levels of thoughts through metacognitive effort. (The practical application of theoretical thinking model). After all, rocket science is not needed to know "how" you feel.

Besides using a different portion of the brain (discussed in the material on the brain and neurotransmitters in Core Area 8), we also mitigate the emotional effects that lead to bodily stress. (Your frontal lobe takes center stage as functional operation rather than the mid-brain emotional center).

Many will say that when they are experiencing the emotions they are "overcome with emotions" and can't control them. I beg to differ and offer this example to make my point-

Managing the damage from emotional reasoning (step 2)

If you are in a car driving down the interstate and a tire blows what do you do? Do you panic and freak out (overcome with emotion) or do you do what you have to in order to safely get off of the road?

If you are in a dangerous situation (life-threatening such as combat or crime scene) do you panic and freak out (overcome with emotion) or do you do what you have to in order to keep yourself and others alive and safe?

Your answer to these questions will serve to determine how you are or are not able to manage your emotions. Consider these answers carefully.

Managing the damage from emotional reasoning (step 3)

If you do not get a good night's sleep or have not had food to eat for a while; how well are you able to handle emotionally-laden problems? Chances are that it is difficult to handle problems and it taxes the person beyond what would otherwise be the case

Along with asking oneself, "WHY I FEEL THE WAY THAT I DO" (rather than WHAT), one has another basic tool that must be used to help them to manage their emotional state and be able to rely on rational, critical-thinking skills instead.

The additional key is to manage emotions involves the practice of "GOOD EMOTIONAL SELF-REGULATING BEHAVIORS"

GOOD EMOTIONAL SELF-REGULATING BEHAVIORS (See Core Area 4 for fuller treatment). Here is an abbreviated view:

In order to gain the necessary advantages to manage emotional problems it is important to have adequate (at minimum) sleep, diet, exercise, meditation and relaxation, and a structured schedule that allows for meaningful activities (work or dedicated interests) which promote good self-esteem and a positive self-concept.

Self-esteem is the ability to feel about oneself- elevated self-esteem is feeling that one is worthwhile, of value, and capable and possessing the same skills as those who they are in contact with and frequently associate with.
Self-concept is how one sees themselves and what they are in their own estimation. This includes their roles and titles in life (the hats that they wear).

Briefly stated Emotional Regulating behaviors include:

#1 Sleep hygiene

- The amount of sleep needed varies with the age of the person as well as the time that one goes to sleep and gets up from sleep. The very young and the very old go to sleep early in the evening with the young sleeping >8/10 hrs. The old also go to bed early but also arise early (advanced sleep cycle).

- The room should be dark to associate the brain with darkness=sleep. There should be NO TV, RADIO, etc. in the room (it becomes another living room otherwise for the psyche). (Brain increases production of melatonin in a dark environment for sleep).

- Avoid napping during the day in order to maintain a stable biological "clock".

- Avoid stimulants (e.g. caffeine, nicotine, and alcohol or drugs) close to bedtime.

- Exercise can promote good sleep as will healthy, physical exertion such as manual labor (gardening or in-house work are examples).

- Food prior to bedtime is problematic to restful sleep as a rule.

- Ensure adequate exposure to natural light during the day to keep the "clock" set and aid melatonin processes.

- Establish a set, structured sleep-wake schedule (have a set sleep time).

- Avoid stressful and serious discussions or arguments when getting ready for sleep.

- There should be clothes associated only with sleep (psychologically associating the clothes with the activity of rest).

- Alcohol consumption does not lead to healthy sleep. You may "pass out" for around 4 to 5 hours but the alcohol will lead to increased excitatory neurotransmitter action in the brain that will prematurely wake the person up with an inability to return to sleep for the necessary amount of hours of night's sleep.

- The time to go to bed and the time to get up is important. It is essential that the times are consistent for the sleep/wake biological clock to be (and remain) set. Otherwise, it will set and reset as the person's routine varies with little consistency being a deterrence to good mental health. See Core Area 4 for an in-depth explanation of the "sleep-wake clock".

#2 Meditation and leisure

The factors typically associated with recreational therapy programming include ensuring that all activities include a physical, mental, spiritual, emotional, and social component whenever possible. Thus, we need to consider our free time and making sure that these aspects are included in our leisure.

The greatest causes of physical ailments include heart attack and stroke both have a proximal cause from stress brought on by emotional dysfunctional behaviors. Leisure is not optional as a source of relaxation and rejuvenation.

Meditation and breathing (diaphragmatic breathing) are also **essential** to relieve the stress that comes from emotions. (See Core Area 4).

Behavioral Activation strategies always have shown through research to be effective in lowering and correcting dysfunction of anxiety and depression by engaging in 1+ hours of personally important leisure activity with others on a daily basis. Not only do we do the activity but we spent time in anticipation of the event and time afterwards reviewing and reliving the time well spent.

This results in a great deal of the day being focused on a positive experience.

#3 The case for a spiritual lifestyle to manage emotional trauma

When you were young and had a big brother or other person who took up for you it made you feel good did it not? It is always nice to know that someone has your back? Having the faith in a Source to be there for you since not a single human can, without fail, always have your best interest in mind is important if not critical for good mental health.

Also, being able to realize that further down the road the Source was a reason for your efforts (to be connected in an eternal state) to be with allows one to look to the future rather than follow the societal rule of "living for the moment". Since there is a future one is not in a place of having their joy crushed when they experience a disappointment in the present. Since the future matters, there is a basic requirement for a spiritual component to one's life.

The end result is that one has much improved coping ability from this mindset often times (by self-report of the one who is engaged in a spiritual lifestyle).

#4 A spiritual awakening – the research supports spirituality

In order to complete my dissertation for my doctorate studies I conducted a research project on the factors associated with long term abstinence from substance abuse and addiction. This is a scientific research study that utilizes a psychological test measure entitles the Spiritual Health Inventory Index.

The most significant fact that I gained from this was that that in all but 1 instance, every person who had long term abstinence stated that they had experienced "a spiritual awakening". They pointed to an understanding that God and addictive substances do not mix. They needed to rely on someone who was greater than themselves because they did not have the ability to overcome their problems on their own. The idea was to place their Source as primary to their recovery (and lives) to ensure a more stable emotional state. If you prefer scientific methods-Here's your sign!

#5 Diet (See Core Area 4 for extensive, detailed treatment)

#6 12-step programming as "free therapy"-(spirituality based)

The most long-lived programming for SA issues is the 12-Step Recovery Program known as AA. At a date more recent, NA was established to allow those who had addiction from drugs (that weren't alcohol related) could attend an environment which they felt was more tailored to their drugs of choice use.

It is reasonable to accept that there was a perceived importance for spirituality to overcome addiction- in essence, one had a dependent (and addictive) personality and formed a reliance on a Higher Power rather than drugs and alcohol. This AA participation for the addict in recovery is essential for routine support.
AA and NA continue to be a primary support source (free treatment that is available practically everywhere) for those dealing with emotional dysregulating behaviors rather than self-medicating with drugs and alcohol. These associations deal with the daily emotional experiences of the addict in recovery.

#7 A Structured Schedule

Clinical experience has provided me with the understanding that when people are active and involved in a daily schedule they function better. They usually take better care of their appearance and hygiene and this is in addition to sleeping better at night (due to not napping during the day and being exhausted from their daily efforts) as well as have a heartier appetite.

Self-esteem is improved when people feel that they are being productive-whether it is by holding down a job or doing a hobby that is their passion. This factor requires a structured schedule that keeps the person focused, energized, and using their physical and mental abilities. This ensures good physical, mental, and emotional health as a byproduct of a structured daily lifestyle.

Emotions-feeling good, versus, Behaviors- being good

Emotions have an effect of stretching the personality to take on life on life's terms. In so doing, life's lessons are learned and the stress of learning those lessons has the function of being a growth exercise. This occurs when the follow up is to employ reason and critical, thinking skills. Otherwise, feeling good mitigates learning those lessons and allows one to feel (emotion) better without being better (behavior).

Behaviors that are based on accomplishing a task rather than allowing one to feel good will lead to happiness due to the satisfaction of being successful. One is able to grow and develop which is a positive long-term experience. Only functioning to feel good (absent being productive and task oriented) does not lead to long-term, truly satisfying happiness). The "rule of thumb" is that the happiness should be derived from a content, satisfied, balanced state of being rather than from a chemical distortion experienced by using drugs. (Opposite ends versus balance is called a bipolar disorder for a reason).

The emotional basis for mental health treatment need

As has been discussed, the majority of treatment is (often) based on treating emotions rather and any other aspect of the functioning of the individual.
As has also been discussed, in part 1 (THINKING), people routinely "take somewhere" what others have been engaged within interpersonal relationships with them express. This leads to a pattern that supports emotional dysregulation and is a poor/dysfunctional basis for personality that appears to be a proximal cause for mental health issues.

Not only do people take it somewhere unrelated to the discussion, the secondary factor continues to be self-medicating or engaging in the multiple options available to distract oneself from reality (media, electronics, sex, drugs/alcohol, food, materialism, etc.). None of these distractions take the place of appropriate mental functioning that is founded on rational, critical-thinking, logical, deductive reasoning absent a reliance on emotions.

A thought about emotion

"The actual, fundamental (and essential) need to be engaged in the conversation was avoided by going somewhere else with the situation. Further, it is frequently the case that the "taking it somewhere" leads to an emotional result. Further, it leads to considering the emotional context negatively for the person thinking of themselves or others in the communicating process. The final straw occurs when the one who has "taken it somewhere" gives the emotion-based judgments a legitimacy for themselves, or about others. In essence, people may be prone to see their emotional considerations of being stupid, ugly, dumb, etc. as the true reality (a "fact") for their lives."

The result of the thoughts based on emotion

When this process becomes the consistent choice and common result of the persons' everyday world-mental illness and dysfunction is to be expected.

Although each of us has a different tolerance level and strength of character integrity, "going to the well" too often will find us impeded and potentially demonstrating dysfunctional mental health as the result of constantly "taking it somewhere". The amount of distress that we able to handle is commonly referred to as the "stress-tolerance level" of the individual. An additional admission that is necessary to add to the equation is that when the individuals do not practice positive self-care practices (good diet, adequate sleep, exercise, meditation, spiritual growth-related activities, and a stable, structured daily schedule) these problems have a greater chance of causing dysfunction.

(2-A)

CORE AREA TWO – DISCUSSION QUESTIONS

(SELF REFLECTION)- Assess Your Tendencies for Emotional-Based, Decision-Making).

1. When you make a decision, how much emphasis of the proposed solution is based on "feeling good"?

2. When you make a decision, how much emphasis of the proposed solution is based on "thinking that they decision is effective"?

3. If you do not have enough sleep or are not eating the right diet, how well are you able to manage emotional stress?

4. Give 5 things that are helpful by having a structured daily schedule, and, why is structure important (or not important)?

5. Provide examples of emotionally-based decisions that you have made that worked out positively long term. (NOT SHORT-TERM, "FEELING GOOD").

6. If you are able to provide positive examples ask yourself if there was a rational, deductive thinking part to that decision? (Realize, thinking should have played a part in the decision-if so-then it wasn't an emotionally-based decision and, instead, was more well-rounded).

7. How many bad sleep hygiene practices to you do?

8. How many good sleep hygiene practices do you do?

9. What are you doing regarding your cognitive functioning when you ask yourself "why" you feel a certain way, versus, your cognitive functioning when you consider "what" you feel?
   (HINT) Core Area 8- The Brain- "Short circuiting emotional expressions-Amygdala". (Sneak peek ahead if you want).

REVIEW QUESTIONS ABOUT THE EMOTIONS CORE AREA MATERIALS- (SKILLS BUILDING)

1. Does the "Ice Cream Sundae" technique make sense to you- Why, or Why Not?

2. Do you think that therapy should be about how you feel mainly, or, about what were you thinking?

3. Can you see the advantage to asking yourself "why" you feel a particular way in situations versus asking yourself "what" you feel?

4. Give 5 examples where your emotional reasoning left you with beliefs about yourself or others that were not based on actual factual information.

CORE AREA THREE
BEHAVIORS (CBT-Step 3)
The TWO TYPES OF BEHAVIORS-

(Those to accomplish an objective – OR – those that focus on continuing to feel good or avoid feeling bad).

LEARNING OBJECTIVE FOR THIS CORE: Observations of human behavior shows me that most people are trying to do one of two things as a motivation for their behavioral actions. They are either- trying to accomplish a task or an objective to reach an improved state or to avoid a penalty. OR- they are trying to continue to feel good, feel better, or discard an unpleasant emotional state.

A basic belief is that feeling good is possible by merely attempting to attain it with direct emotional satisfaction, instead, true happiness occurs often when tasks or objectives are meet thereby allowing the person to experience a resultant, deeply personal self-satisfaction due to their success. The follow-up includes elevated self-esteem and happiness from their success (without drugs or other substances).

Behavior A- Trying to achieve and succeed at task as a reason for behavior-

Central to achievement and success is to utilize facts, information, data, or figures to satisfy the steps needed to realize goals and ambitions. This is arrived at through reason based on deductive, critical-thinking skills and logical-based abilities. This is a true test of the intellect and dedication of the individual to achieve the ambitions which are at the basis for their work and efforts. How one feels about those facts or figures does not change their importance or status. (2 plus 2 is always 4, if you feel differently it does not matter). The person's behavior reflects the application of the truth of the situation to succeed, failure to apply facts and figures with a thinking process, dooms the person to an ultimate, end-point, failure.

VERSUS

Behavior B- Maintaining a good feeling or discarding a bad feeling as the motivation for behavior.

(Either one succeeds with a task oriented behavior to feel good as a byproduct of their effort or, they engage in a primary behavior to maintain a good feeling or to get rid of unpleasant feelings or emotions as their motivation for behavior). **When they do this, they are forced to manipulate their environment** so that they can achieve their goal of feeling good. This presents the basis for much behavior and is becoming a common, routine basis for secular behavior. This is in response to the "rules" for the modern day that "one must feel good and, if one is not feeling good, one must be making efforts to feel good".

(This short circuits the lessons learned from working through unpleasant situations to completion of the tasks to realize the satisfaction from accomplishment by effort to reach goals).

BEHAVIORAL TECHNIQUES

The individual who chooses to manipulate their environment to maintain a good feeling or to discard an unpleasant feeling has to have a mechanism to accomplish this objective. (A failure to address their problems head-on is the result). They, in effect, **use behavioral techniques to accomplish their objective to "feel good".** The primary purpose or utility to these techniques is to accomplish the goal of feeling good (emotional satisfaction) thus, they are of a subjective nature that is not based necessarily on objective truth. In these instances, the use of opinions and persuasion are more valued than facts and information of a truth-oriented nature. (Right and wrong do not seem to matter often times).

What follows is a partial list that includes 21 different identified behavioral techniques frequently employed. This is not an all-encompassing list and is the results of over 20 years of my behavioral observations of clients in treatment. **(Dictionary definition followed by an example-there are other examples that you may offer for each).**

#1 Marginalizing

"To relegate to a powerless or unimportant position within a society or group".
In order to give legitimacy to opinions or attitudes that support a belief of the individual or the group of individuals with which this person is a member, others are marginalized to support their needs and objectives being met rather than those who are the marginalized people(s).

#2 Minimize

"To reduce or keep to a minimum. To underestimate intentionally."
This tactic is used to disregard the complaints or disagreement of anyone who does not share their wishes or who could get in the way of the person who is using minimizing techniques to attain a positive emotional state.

#3 Avoiding

"To keep away from. To prevent the occurrence or effectiveness".
Truth and reality are discarded in the event that it gets in the way of personal experiencing of pleasure such that a consideration for the potential of harm (addiction, overdose, or penalty) is dealt with, absent rational concern.

#4 Ignoring

"To refuse to take notice, to reject as ungrounded".
Even when the behavior may negatively affect self or others this is not enough of a reason to avert the behavior. The need to feel good outweighs being good. This goal of feeling good does not allow any room for considering the threat to life and health that the behavioral technique's use may cause.

#5 Denial

"To refuse to admit the truth or reality, disavowing truth without a basis for the assertion, a negation of logic".
This is at the core of addiction and is the first thing that must be overcome to even consider the damage and danger from use of drugs and alcohol. This is the techniques which allows a mental disorder to gain strength within the person and root in their psyche rather than addressing the initial problems which would have disallowed the disorder from developing.

#6 Perverting

"To cause to turn away from what is good, true, or moral".
Seemingly harsh in reality, it is not realized fully by the one(s) who typically use it- their desire to feel good and get their needs met is given greater weight than doing good and delusional thinking is preferred to base reality or common sense.

#7 Contorting

"To twist something out of shape".
To give an explanation or excuse for something that is used to get off of the hook or justify what has been done. This is self-explanatory and is the means by which most of self-serving behaviors that promote feeling good are couched in by the explainer.

#8 Confusing

"Frustrate. To disturb in mind and purpose. To fail to differentiate".

If one can antagonize others long enough then they will give up is a strategy that is arrived at by the behavioral technique of confusing the issues, facts, circumstances, etc. This is a common technique used in many circumstances- law, politics, marketing, interpersonal relationships, etc.

#9 Manipulate

"To control or play upon artfully, unfairly, or to an insidious benefit or advantage for the practitioner".
This is typically carried out by someone intentionally and with a general lack of respect for the rights of others. The need to feel good is such that a respectful regard for others is avoided due to the interest in realizing or achieving the goal to feel good.

#10 Over-valuation

"To assign an excessive worth to something".
This is the basis for the feeling good philosophy. The things that pass for worthless I don't understand was a statement is a rock-and-roll song of the 70s and this is synonymous with the behavioral technique of over-valuing that which is able to make one feel good even if it is detrimental to self or others.

#11 Under-valuation

"To treat as if it is of little worth".
This is common as a lack of regard for traditional values that hold worth to cultural ideals such as personal responsibility, individual independence, and the virtues of which patience, humility, honesty, trustworthiness, and other values are held in low standing if they get in the way of feeling good.

#12 Justification

"The act of process of validating self or decisions and actions".
In the essence of behavioral technique's application it is often an excuse that is dressed up by often using unrelated or unimportant facts to make OK that which is not logical or appropriate.

#13 Excusing

"To remove blame for, to weigh as trivial, and expression of regret for doing something".
The central thing that is evident is that it is necessary to understand whether the individual is genuine and if the thing being excused is really trivial or is important

but being minimized to not serve as a way of stopping the seeking of feeling good or avoiding feeling bad.

#14 Blaming

"To find fault or hold responsible".
Typically, this is used to shift the attention away from the one who is avoiding being thwarted in their efforts to find a pleasurable state, absent pain and anxiety. This is a standard technique used by those who abuse substances as a reason for their use. They attribute the use of the substances because of someone else who they invariably claim are "the cause" for their use.

#15 Arguing

"To give reason for or against something, to contend against something in words". I have seen frequently that individuals will use arguments as a means of employing other behavioral techniques such as confusion, contorting, perverting, etc. and often have the purpose of wearing down the other party so that they can achieve their ends. This allows one to continue to do as they wish or to change courses to achieve their pleasure related goals.

#16 Ruminating

"To go over in the mind repeatedly and often slowly".
This is a behavioral technique that I was encouraged to avoid as a youth and I have come to realize that it is a basis for the development of anxiety and anxiety-related disorders. It can be demonstrated in numbers in repetitive thinking (3s, 4s, etc.) as they relate to behavior and the anxiety that results when the ruminating is not allows to go on can be the source of much interpersonal problems. (Anxiety increases due to lack of fulfillment).

#17 Dismissal

"To reject any serious consideration of. To remove from service".
When the one who is being challenged for their behavior responds it is typically in this fashion. If he can dismiss the arguments, challenges, or avoid facing reality then he can continue to feel good absent any regard for anything that can get in the way of feeling good.

18 Insulting

"To treat with insolence, indignity, or contempt. To behave with pride and arrogance".

When you see the opposite sides to the political spectrum this is the predominate trait to describe their responses to each other. On the individual level, when one does not cave in to their arguments of the one who is concerned about feeling good, all they may have to offer (absent facts and only based on opinions) is to insult the other one who will not agree with them.

19 Criticize

"To find fault with or point out the faults of others".
When the person who is attempting to maintain their state has few legitimate objections to the other person(s) then all that is left is to personalize the situation and often attack the other by labels and generalizations. They do this to criticize the other one so that they can dumb down the discussion away from facts and information and to a personal level (with no facts and truth).

20 Lie

"To make an untrue statement with the intention to deceive. To make or give a misleading impression".
This is a fundamental trait factor that develops early in adolescent to avoid being honest concerning behaviors that they know to be wrong. The idea is that their parents would object, thus, a lie is required. Once the skill to lying is honed then it becomes a standard means of forwarding their agenda- as long as they feel good it is OK. The problem is that they are aware by their consciousness that the lie causes bad personal feelings so it actually does just the opposite for a time. If continued unabated then the guilt is lessened until such time as they may confuse lie with truth in their own psyche.

21 Distort

"To twist out of the true meaning; to cause to be seen unnaturally".
If one can confuse then they can avoid detection due to an inability to actually address the issue(s). If one can twist the true meaning as to what is at stake the possibility of detection or correction is lost. A look at the typical, present-day political climate is a good example of this behavioral technique, in action. Regardless of which side of the political landscape one is on, they will use this definition to describe what they see in the political arena as it relates to their perspective regarding distortion.

Behavioral development for Addiction and Mental Health Issues- a Perspective by the Author

There appears to be a pattern that explains the basic developmental pattern of behavior as it relates to the individual in treatment. It has a total of 7 stages as it regards the development of many mental health and most substance abuse issues. This is also a great tool to understand the basic development prior to a fuller treatment of the developmental stage models (Erickson's, Piaget's, Kohlberg's, Family Systems, etc. that are discussed in Core Area 6). (The following model happens on a chronological basis as well as in individual situations of personal growth, change, and development).

These stages are, briefly; awareness, curiosity, acceptance, experimentation, habit/social, addiction/mental health diagnosis, recovery/death/rehabilitation. These stages may be re-experienced in some cases (addiction, recovery, and/or the final stage). My development of this stage model does not attempt to address all aspects of the human being yet is useful to understand the basic behavioral progression and the alternative roads taken.

Awareness

The infant and, then later, small child observes their world and develops some basic understandings about life and those in their family and surroundings. This is how they understand what is "normal" (Core Area 5) as most do not see those things that they are exposed to in any other way-if this is what mom and dad are doing then it must be OK. After all, this is their parents and they are never wrong. It is only when they become exposed to their peers and they can compare notes on how their peer's parents are acting can they see if things are the same or different-they still have to make the decision as to what is "normal".

Curiosity

Part of the observation and awareness process involves making perspective and attitude of what they see, hear, feel, taste, and smell. When they see and hear laughter it seems only appropriate to determine that what is going on is funny and pleasurable. When they see pain-it is something to be avoided, etc. Part of this weighing and measuring process is in play due to curiosity that makes them aware of the environment-when they see adults drinking alcoholic beverages, smell pot smoke, or watch unusually behaviors from drug use they draw a conclusion about this. They often go to the next state with-

Acceptance

They develop a list of what is good, bad, desirable, undesirable, liked, disliked, or not important. This is the acceptance process and involves all aspects of their world from food, to substances, behaviors, speech, looks and appearances, dress, hygiene, etc. This is the list from which they will begin experimenting upon when reaching mid-adolescence. This is when they taste freedom from parental guidance and oversight that has often been hands on up until this point. This is the beginning of becoming an adult, and then the stage begins known as-

Experimentation

This is when they find out where they are and who they are, who they like and dislike, and learn through experimentation about substances, sex, materialism, cultural practices, etc. This is the beginning of the Friday night parties with friends before and after high school sporting events with the social elements associated with those events. They grow into their world with these interactions and the day-to-day classroom exchanges. This is a time of trying out new things and when social protocol teaches them the "rules" (Core Area 1) that lead to problems that must, later, be overcome with maturity. This is the point which leads to the introduction of intimate relations and later results in children from the unions often begun during this stage (traditional based).

Socially Only [or] Habit

As the adolescent goes to college or sets off on his/her own (with their own residence) they will develop patterns of behavior and how they schedule their lives. These schedules will become standard practice and will dictate their lives in many meaningful ways. Their personal preferences and their social circles will dictate whether they behave socially with restraint or develop substance use (or other distraction habits) that may escalate into an addiction or problem mental health disorder based upon ineffective coping and functional strategies in their own lives.

Addiction & Mental Health Diagnosis

Understand that some will remain in the habit or pre-habit stage of behavioral development (for a time-or- reduce use to be socially restrained) and not experience addiction or mental health issues. However, the follow-up to experimentation, then habit, is frequently-addiction. Likewise, ineffectual coping strategies or the results of defining abnormal as "normal" due to their environmental influences will result in much mental health issue(s). I have often heard it said in training that, "if you show me an anxious child I will show you an anxious mother or father" (modeled behavior that has been assimilated and allowed to reach a problem state in late adolescence, early adulthood). There is a significant connection with the environment but the individual stages of acceptance, experimentation, and habit all lead to the final point of arriving at addiction and mental health concerns.

NOTE* It has been theorized through research that over 70% of those who have addiction also have Personality Disorders typically due to underdeveloped, or dysfunctional, personality development during adolescence. See Core Area 5.

Recovery/death/rehabilitation

These are the potential outcomes to the substance use disorder or the mental health diagnosis with the granted understanding that many, if not most, continue in the previous stage (Addiction and Mental Health Disorders). At some point, these possibilities play out for the majority of those who do not take steps to curb their use. The preferred progression that serves as the basis for treatment is to assist the client to recover their previous health and shed the troubles associated with addiction and mental health pain.

Unfortunately, overdoses occur as the addict continues an attempt to rediscover that first high that they can never replicate. Many attend rehabilitation treatment centers for multiple treatments before they achieve extended abstinence. The virtue of "hope" continues to keep those involved in the rehabilitative process giving effort to achieve abstinence for the addict/or mentally disordered as they engage in treatment.

Note: The goal remains for recovery throughout the progression of this model.

(3-A)

CORE AREA THREE- SELF-DISCOVERY EXERCISE
(Refer to the Core Area 3 text to review each technique).

A. Behavioral Techniques

Marginalized	Minimize	Avoiding	Ignoring
Denial	Perverting	Contorting	Confusing
Manipulate	Over-Valuation	Under-Valuation	Justification
Excusing	Blaming	Arguing	Ruminating
Dismissal	Insulting	Criticize	Lie
Distort			

1. Ask yourself how you have used each behavioral technique to provide emotional satisfaction?

2. Have you fully processed the way, or ways, in which behavioral techniques allow you to avoid dealing with problems? (Consider this on an ongoing basis as you face new problems).

(REMEMBER- These serves as ways to avoid dealing effectively with life and facing unpleasant, but necessary situations and experiences for growth and positive development).

B. Behavioral Model for Development

a. Awareness
b. Curiosity
c. Acceptance
d. Experimentation
e. Socially Only (or) Habit
f. Addiction & Mental Health Disorders
g. Recovery/death/rehabilitation

3. Personally, review your life experiences as they relate to the behavioral model provided in the Core Area 3 text.

4. Give examples of what things happened during each of these stages relating to your life experience. How did they impact your development?

CORE AREA FOUR
EMOTIONAL SELF-REGULATING-
Taking Charge of Your Life So That It Does Not Take Charge of You

A Common-Sense Approach to Good Mental Health
An Overview of Emotional Self-Regulation

It is difficult to control our emotions, especially when we lack sleep, food, or other normally occurring needs being routinely met on an ongoing basis.

When we have mental health issues such as anxiety, depression, adjustment-related issues, or manic behaviors we have even greater difficulty dealing with the problems that occur in our daily lives. When we do not engage in a structured, daily life we have time to ruminate over our problems (which further exacerbates them)-making them increasingly more troublesome.

These issues lead to a continually increasing, never-ending series of poor mental health functioning and, frequently, we add an additional mental health problem. Examples include addiction from choosing to self-medicate with drugs and alcohol to numb or distort their thinking. This behavior denies attempts to actively address their mental health issues-the cycle continues. Going even further, when these things occur we may use compensatory strategies such as eating or isolating and these amplify psychologically damaging feeling of low self-esteem or devaluing of self. It just continues absent corrective actions such as those identified in this core area material.

An Explanation for the Urgency to an Address of the Topic

A learned statement for required behaviors that I realized while in combat-era military service in the early 1970's was that:

"It is hard to remember that you came to drain the swamp when you are up to your waist in alligators". This is an explanation for why we did, what we did, when it did not directly apply to what we were attempting to accomplish. It has always stuck with me. I have found that there is a certain wisdom to this statement and it has multiple applications.

As the statement applies to this presentation...

We may be trying to deal with mental health issues directly by addressing the diagnosed dysfunction regarding thinking, feeling, and behavior. However, if someone is unable to eat, sleep, rest, or manage daily needs then talking about

mental health models or treatment options will not be well received. This is not the focus of their attention. *They are only trying to avoid the alligators.*

1. LACK OF SLEEP-A Cause & Result of Mental Health Issues

Substance abuse and MH issues leads to irregular and unrestful sleep and this may spiral out of control into the development of physical or mental health concerns. Anxiety robs the person of a restful state as the person worries well into the night rather than being able to go to sleep peacefully. Their mind will not stop racing thus their active thinking serves to torture their attempts to rest.

Irregular work schedules, alternating shift work, addiction, and periods of unemployment where day time naps occur all serve to disturb the circadian sleep-wake cycle. This is certainly to the detriment of the person thereby increasing mental health concerns. The lack of sleep goes forward to rob the person of good mental health and physical health so that they experience continually increasing poor and unsafe functional status. This is an increasingly damaging cycle.

Understanding the Sleep-Wake Cycle to Realize the Need for Structure in our Lives

A simplified version of the discussion of the sleep-wake cycle follows so that you can see how we operate regarding our internal "clock". (This will make the need for structure apparent).

Our sleep-wake cycle (circadian rhythm) is made up essentially of 3 parts-a 16 hour wake state and 2 approximately four (4) hour sleep periods known as the non-REM (Rapid Eye Movement) sleep state of 4 hours and the REM sleep state of 4 hours (8 hour sleep state in total).

The easiest way to understand the brain in these various states is to understand that the cerebral cortex (outer part of the brain) is active with sensory and movement activities occurring during the 16 awake hours, and to a lessor degree, during the REM 4-hour sleep state (although it does not integrate the various brain functions while in this REM sleep phase extensively). During the 4-hour non-REM state of sleep there is very little, if any, activity in the cerebral cortex.

The initial signal to awaken the cycle beginning with the 16 hours of wake period begins with the light hits the photogenic cells in the iris of the eye. This activates a signal to the suprachiasmatic nucleus (from the optic nerve) and then to various cells that have SRN neuron action within those various organs and sites (as well as in the brain). These nuclei oscillate during the wake-sleep period and regulate the melatonin from the pineal gland located behind the eye to where the signal is sent to begin this nuclei oscillation process. This control over the melatonin is done to orchestrate the activities of the brain and organs during the wake state.

Melatonin starts its production at the advent of sleep with the pineal gland reaching the fullest production of melatonin around 3-4AM but then it is regulated (during the day) by these SRN nuclei. Near the end of the 16-hour awake period, adenosine (used to medically treat erratically fast heartrates also) is produced by glandular activity to start the switch over from the 16-hour wake period to the beginning of the sleep time known as going through the "sleep gate". The melatonin has reached its peak of activity through the nuclei direction prior to this adenosine production. The adenosine production serves the purpose of slowing down the excitatory neurotransmitters (especially norepinephrine and epinephrine) so that the person will not remain "keyed up". This is so that they can fall off to sleep.

The person falls off to sleep typically around the end, or in near proximity, of the 16-hour wake period. (They enter what is known as the homeostatic sleep regulation phase of the sleep-wake cycle). This homeostatic sleep regulation phase consists of the two, 4-hour, periods of sleep. This first 4 -hour period (non-REM phase) is one or repair and reproduction/maintenance of the cellular structures in the body and brain primarily. Then the second 4-hour period (REM phase) occurs and melatonin production reaches its peak production in the pineal gland by this point. Also, non-integrated brain functional activities may occur at this time (REM) in the cerebral cortex. Of note, if the adenosine production is insufficient due to problems with the brain, then night-terror, sleepwalking, insomnia, or nightmares can occur. (It is suggested that the lack of sufficient mitigation of the excitatory neurotransmitters brain activity by the earlier adenosine production is the cause). Then, light hits the photogenic cells in the iris and the cycle is reset and the "clock" restarts for another day.

The point being after giving this information is that the sleep-wake process is very complicated. Failure to keep structure to this cycle is damaging and potentially destructive to good mental health.

THE COMPLICATED NATURE OF THIS INTERNAL "CLOCK" IS THE PRIMARY REASON THAT THIS WRITER IS EMPHATIC ABOUT THE IMPORTANCE OF MAINTAINING A STRUCTURED DAILY SCHEDULE THAT RESPECTS THE BODY CLOCK WHILE KEEPING IT IN CONSISTENT OPERATION.

2. **LEARNING TO BREATHE- An Additional Health-Related Dysfunction**

One of the first things I ask clients who suffer from anxiety to be aware of is their lack of adequate breathing when they are experiencing a panic-related event or have generalized anxiety that is at a severe point. The typical factor is that they are not breathing- except for, or only, very shallowly.

Most people do not breathe properly. A way of supporting this statement is to ask you to consider why you have those infrequently deep breaths during the day when you "sigh". The fact is that; your body builds up carbon dioxide from spent oxygen that remains in the lungs due to not being adequately expelled by deep breathing. Carbon dioxide is a poison and is a contributing factor to stress of the body. This plays out with secretion of cortisol that has major implications for stroke, heart disease, and immune dysfunction. Your body is only reacting.

Along with the carbon dioxide, a hormone known as cortisol is secreted in the brain from stress which causes headaches. **(Cortisol can cause tissue damage as well- particularly so with Type "A" Personalities which operate with more stress (thus more cortisol) daily, typically so).** The anxiety that causes the cortisol also causes lactate to be secreted in the muscle tissue of the body to make you weak, sore, and tired. (This is due to the tension in the muscles due to anxiety and panic-related stress). A greatly contributing factor is lack of breathing properly while taking steps to de-stress thru relaxing and learning better coping strategies.

Diaphragmatic Breathing-We Can Learn By Observing a Baby's Breathing. See Worksheet 2 **(WK-2)** for Checklist Approach to Mastery (At end of Manual).

Typically, only a baby breathes properly (they use their belly as a part of the process for breathing in and out of oxygen).
The idea is that the air is drawn all the way down to the diaphragm (base of the belly entrance) so that the entire lung (all lobes in both lungs) receives a steady supply of fresh oxygen. Then, when the carbon dioxide is expelled, the belly is essentially "sucked in" to squeeze the lungs in to push out this carbon dioxide. Only realize that if you have a hospital stay you will notice that the staff are particularly interested in your "blood sat-oxygen level" which, with higher oxygen levels, leads to better health.

In everyday life, more oxygen makes for healthier body tissues (muscles, brain matter, etc.) Also, the nutrients that our body consumes (food and liquids) are better processed, used, and filtered by our bodies by the availability of oxygen-rich blood.

Improving Sleep by Diaphragmatic Breathing and the Irony of a Restless Mind

Meditation- it allows the mind and body to rest by making a conscious effort of self-managing personal awareness of functioning.

People often misunderstand the concept of meditation and ascribe the picture of a monk or lotus position to meditating. For some, the result is that they do not further consider the benefits to meditation for their improved health. The central point that I have always attempted to make with individuals who claim that they can't sleep (usually point to a restless mind) is, **DON'T TRY TO STOP YOUR MIND FROM WORKING-JUST REDIRECT YOUR WORKING MIND TOWARDS ALLOWING YOU TO SLEEP RESTFULLY BY FOCUSING ON YOUR BREATHING.**

Let your mind work for you rather than against you. It is easy, and the key is to focus the restless mind towards the goal of self-awareness to achieve sleep. There is a simple way to accomplish this (I have utilized it for over 45 years and it works!) Here is how it works-

Meditating for Consistent Restful Sleep (Progressive Relaxation)

Step 1- get in a comfortable position so that you can fall off to sleep (or relax).

Step 2 – begin Diaphragmatic Breathing and concentrate the mind on the entire breathing process and the air going into the body (belly out-not chest), being expelled (belly in), and the restful feeling that comes over you. Once you have gotten into a rhythm-

Step 3 – Concentrate on each part of the body (in order) and concentrate on taking all tension and muscle tightness out of each area in turn. Meanwhile, continue concentration on your breathing (do not hyperventilate).

Step 4 – Concentrate on the fingers and toe (taking out the tension and relaxing them), then the hands and feet (same process), then the legs and arms (same process), then the trunk (belly and chest), then the neck and back, and lastly, the facial muscles and a total concentration on the body for relaxing totally.

Additional Rules to Observe (during Meditation) and Expected Benefits that follow-

If you lose concentration or have an itch that you scratch, start the entire process over again from the beginning until such time as you can make it through the whole technique.

Guess what-you probably won't make it through the whole technique because you will usually already be asleep.

When you begin doing this process it will not work well initially, but, do not quit- after a few weeks you will begin to realize benefits and have improvements to your sleep. A little at first but every increasing until after 4 to 6 weeks most people realizing good, restful sleep.

This technique must be used EVERY night or it will not be able to help well.
This process SHOULD be used for 15 minutes on reoccurring intervals. One should repeat this process at least x4 times at minimum during the day (includes when going to sleep) so that stress and mental health issues can be managed during the day. Proper breathing has the belly expand when air enters the lungs-not the

chest expanding AND belly being "sucked in" when exhaling to squeeze out carbon dioxide. (Just like when you want to look skinny to impress someone).

Additionally-Regarding the stress-relieving process; incorporate a basic "Stress Inoculation Strategy" (rules for simplifying life). Some rules I suggest to my clients include:

- If it doesn't matter say 5 years from now, don't sweat it and just let it go.
- If it is a good idea now, it will be a good idea in a week or two (to take time to avoid rash decisions that may prove to be harmful later).
- If it does not address your basic needs of food, shelter, temperature comfort, sleep, and safety/security-leave it alone. (It is always a good spiritual principle to be happy with what you already have rather than a desire/drive for materialism).
- At the end of the day-when you are lying in bed reviewing your day prior to sleep, if you did things properly or succeeded then be satisfied. If not, and more needs to be done or changed, take care of it tomorrow. (Worrying about it at night will not get it done-fix it tomorrow when you begin another day).
- Don't expect others to live up to your beliefs or demands. Other than your security and the safety/security of those you love-let others be responsible for yourself. (Stop trying to be the general manager of the universe).

(See Stress Inoculation Checklist at the back of Manual- (WK-3) Worksheet 3.

3. DIET DOES MATTER- Helping your Brain to Function for Good Mental Health

Your body needs amino acids to, in turn, produce neurotransmitters (chemicals) that allow your brain to function. When the neurotransmitters are "firing" properly, then things go smoothly- when you have mental health issues this is not happening with regularity.

The proteins (amino acids) need for neurotransmitter maintenance, operation, and reproduction are found in meats, egg, dairy, and various amounts and types from vegetables and fruits. Grains, nuts, and spices also have benefits as well.

Some very important amino acids that fulfill the needs of a healthy brain include Tyrosine, Tryptophan, and Taurine. Without sufficient amounts of these amino acids there is certainty that dysfunctional behaviors will occur due the inability of the brain to operate as intended.

Here is a brief breakdown of how these 5 amino acids (that serve to make proteins for the body/brain) are available-

Taurine, Tryptophan, and Tyrosine-Amino Acid Building Blocks for the Brain

Foods that produce taurine include egg, fish, red meat, and dairy products such as cheese and milk. This amino acid stabilizes the cell membrane of the brain (also allows them to communicate better). Stress, alcohol consumption, and a vegetarian diet will significantly inhibit the benefits of taurine.

Foods that produce tryptophan include brown rice, cottage cheese, peanuts, soy protein, and turkey. Milk, when warmed, releases tryptophan as well. Tryptophan produces serotonin in the brain which elevates mood and works against depression (lack of serotonin is associated with depression).

Tyrosine is produces from almonds, avocados, bananas, lima beans, pumpkin/sesame seeds, and especially- yogurt, cheese, and milk. Tyrosine elevates alertness, concentration, motivation, and retention of new memories/long-term memory operations. It also helps produce thyroid hormone thyroxine and the pituitary hormone norepinephrine. These treat depression by making more dopamine and norepinephrine available. Additionally, it stops hypothyroidism (lower rate of metabolism of foods) for ideal body weight as well as producing melatonin (an aid in sleep and mood).

Additional Amino Acids to Consider for Neurotransmitter Production and Maintenance

Phenylalanine (which, along with Tyrosine) builds the "fight or flight" neurotransmitters (dopamine, epinephrine (adrenaline), and norepinephrine).
Too little may cause a lack of ability to experience pleasure (anhedonia), confusion, emotional agitation, depression, and other significant problems. It can be found in lean beef, shellfish, fowl, and soy products.

Glutamine (leads to production of GABA (Gamma-Amino Butyric Acid)). This is essential for production of the moderating neurotransmitter that curbs anxiety, racing thoughts, and panic (to name a few issues resolved). Can be found in lean beef, pork, sesame and sunflower seeds, and fowl.

*NOTE: The body needs approximately 22 amino acids of which 8 for adults, and 9 for children, cannot be synthesized within the body and must, therefore, come from nutritional sources.

What some Foods really do for the Brain
Eggs (yolk), soybean, wheat germ and organ meats (e.g. liver) help thought functioning and memory functioning. This, in turn, defends against cognitive and memory decline making them even more important as one ages.

Fish (tyrosine) is responsible for dopamine production that gives a mental boost and promotes alertness and activity. Eating these foods will allow greater oxidization of fruit and vegetables which, in turn, help the dopamine using neurons.

Spinach is a chief producer of Folic Acid which is essential for neurotransmitters to process norepinephrine and serotonin. An absence of Folic Acid is linked to depression. Parsley is a great source of Folic Acid as well.

The general fact that must be understood by a brief look at foods for the brain is that they allow the neurotransmitters to function effectively; thus good mental health. The types of neurotransmitters and what they are responsible for are-

Neurotransmitters-The workers that make it all happen

Excitatory Neurotransmitters- Norepinephrine, Epinephrine, Histamine, and Glutamate (too much of these results in Anxiety, PTSD, and/or Bipolar Mania).

Inhibitory Neurotransmitters- Serotonin, GABA, Endorphins. (Good levels aid in calming and relaxing but too little of these result in depression).

Both Excitatory and Inhibitory- Dopamine and acetylcholine (Ach).
When drugs or medications are taken they do one of four basic things to the neurotransmitters in the brain-nothing else for the most part. They either are an agonist, partial agonist, antagonist, or partial antagonist. This means that they either amp up greatly, amp up above "normal", lower below "normal", or decrease or close to cease the activity of the neurotransmitter. The theoretical goal of psychotropic medications is to return the neurotransmitter to the "normal" operating level in the middle place of the continuum (neither above nor below).

Causes of Neurotransmitter Malfunction, Disruption, Deficit, and Imbalances

Alcohol, drugs, and nicotine.
Sugar and caffeine (also- white flour, junk food, diets that are low in protein or high in complex carbohydrates).
Environmental toxins (includes cleaning chemicals, hygiene products with additives, and air fresheners).
Chronic stress (especially when exercise, meditation, and relaxation strategies that counter stress are absent). This absence significantly negatively affects emotionally self-regulating efforts.
Genetics (bipolar, depression, schizophrenia, anxiety often run in family groups).
Nutritional deficits (absence of vitamins and minerals) as well as allergies.

FOODS AS THE BASIS FOR GOOD NEUROTRANSMITTER HEALTH

A. Power Foods are Helpful for Physical and Mental Well-Being

Power foods are those specific foods that give more energy that what is required to chew, digest, and use them by your body and brain. The general idea behind providing a consideration of power foods is based on the idea that they give the "biggest bang for the buck".

The list, in brief, includes Cranberries, Long-Grain Rice, Corn, Pears, Coconut, Parsley, Bananas, Mushrooms, Avocados, Chickpeas, Onions, and Olive Oil.

Cranberries are high in Vitamin C, prevent urinary infections, prevent stomach ulcers, carry away radicals and toxins from the body and inhibit blood clots while increasing blood flow to the heart. They are high in anti-oxidants and play a role in cancer prevention.

Long-Grain rice has a low GI factor (keeps away hunger longer than white rice), high in Thiamin (Vitamin B1) increasing memory and keeps blood sugar levels down (good for diabetes).

Corn is high in Vitamin A, rich in phosphorus (for bones), low in calories and carbohydrates that are easy to digest, and aids in healing kidney dysfunction while lowering cholesterol. It is low in fat and contains Thiamine B vitamin.

Pears are rich in fructose and glucose (energy source), have anti-oxidant properties, relieve constipation, are naturally anti-inflammatory, high in pectin, lower cholesterol, lower the risk of age-related macular degeneration, and protect women from post-menopausal breast cancer. Also-rich in Folate (Vitamin B6).

Coconuts are low in sugar yet high in amino acids. Rich in pantothenic acid (good for hair), fiber, and phosphorous, potassium, magnesium, and calcium.

Parsley- rich in Vitamin K (clotting agent), Vitamin A, Folic Acid, Iron, and has more Vitamin C than oranges and apples. Opens clogged lungs, prevents colon cancer, neutralizes carcinogens, protects against rheumatoid arthritis, removes gall stones, therapeutic for optic nerve, and is beneficial for the nervous system.

Bananas- high in potassium, rich in selenium (prevents colds and flu), and is rich in some trace minerals.

Mushrooms- fat free, stops or prevent some cancers, control blood pressure, high in potassium, and contain both selenium and vitamin E.

Chickpeas- has 2 rare trace minerals (Molybdenum and manganese), rich in amino acid tryptophan, great for diabetes, and detoxes sulfites from the body.

Avocados- prevent prostate cancer, seek out pre-cancerous cells, protect against macular degeneration and cataracts, prevents cell aging, and is high in oleic acid which prevents breast cancer.

Onions- better than garlic for preventing bronchial spasms and opening bronchial constrictions of the lungs. Rich in quercetin and phenols to cleanse the blood.

Olive Oil- Reduces blood pressure and inhibits the growth of some cancers. They also have benefits for controlling diabetes. They are rich in monounsaturated fat, chlorophyll-like carotenoid, and Vitamin E. Can significantly reduce high blood pressure. It stops the hardening of the arteries, LDL (cholesterol) is broken down and washed away by the olive oil due to heavily oxygenating the blood.

B. **Fat Burning and Calorie Crunchers (Assisting in Achieving Body Shape for Personal Feelings of Fitness and Culturally Encouraged Physical/Body Health).**

NOTE: (Psychological sense of well-being is important to good mental health. Often time, cultural ideas of body shape/type mean that individuals often pursue particular body themes. (Strength with muscle mass-men OR slim/trim-women).

Tomatoes- contain a Japanese discovered compound known as 9-OXO-ODA that has been identified as a significant fat burner when eaten as a part of regular diet.

Beans- a basic staple for weight loss while regulating blood sugar and helping digestion (a fiber). Black Beans can be substituted for bread or rice and are often an additional side available on many restaurant menus.

Lentils- high in fiber to assist with weight loss while keeping blood sugar from spiking.

Asparagus- a diuretic (stops fluid retention) while detoxing the body to assist in removal of toxins and waste. It also feeds the stomach gut bacteria (probiotics).

Avocados- known as the "most effective loss snack" due to mood-boosting Vitamin B while lowering the stress hormone, cortisol. This food also helps stop the stomach from having clinging fat body formations.

Broccoli- low fat while filling up the person thus results in eating less typically. (Avoid the cheese).

Spinach- low in calories while filling up the person. Contains folic acid which is essential to process foods to produce proteins for serotonin (for the brain).

Apples, Pears, Oranges, Bananas are all high in fiber which aids in metabolism- they are fat burning like most all acidic or thermo-heat producing foods/spices.

Sweet Potatoes- they have fewer calories than white potatoes. They also have the slow carb effect which keeps the person full longer while maintaining a steady blood sugar level. They lower insulin resistance and prevent calories from turning to fat.

Oats- They have been tried and tested over many generations to keep the person fuller longer through the morning to lunch by boosting metabolism while "sticking to your ribs" (old-fashion explanation). Leads to less snacking-less calories.

Whole Grains instead of white breads and pastries. People that consume three (3) or more servings of whole grains per day have 10% less body fat than 3 or more like-sized servings of white breads and pastries per day (on average). Whole grains are essential due to the transfer of the tryptophan in the whole grains to the production of serotonin as well as being a good source of magnesium (deficits in this lead to anxiety).

Eggs are a complete protein as they are said to contain all (or most all) of the amino acids necessary for the person to live. The dietary guidelines found in preparation for this book indicate that one-a-day is appropriate (hard boiled, rather than fried).

Chicken breast (skinless white meat) is high in protein and low in fat and is considered superior quality of protein than dark meat, chicken. However, dark meat chicken has a 1/3 more iron and 3 times the zinc (builds immune system).

A lean Pork tenderloin typically has less fat content than a skinless Chicken breast.

Peanut Butter has "good" fat and is rich in protein. However, organic varieties are less potentially addictive rich (organic peanut butter usually only has sea salt).

Finally, those foods rich in beta-carotene and lycopene when preferred for one's diet. They lead to smaller waist sizes and lower body fats. These foods include apricots, broccoli, carrots, collard greens, pumpkin, spinach, and sweet onions.

Since Vitamin A, C, and E (antioxidants) are theoretically necessary to avoid aging-related brain damage from free radicals it is important to consider having these foods added to daily diet. (Brain cell molecular structure where one of the two typically found electrons is missing leads to the one electron trying to "steal" another molecule's electron. This is the essential cause and process of free radical impact on cellular structure). Antioxidants supply the additional electron to combat the chain reaction breakdown of the electron molecular battle in essence.

*Antioxidant rich foods include-
Blueberries, broccoli, grapefruit, kiwi, oranges, peppers (aid in stomach health by killing bad bacteria in moderation while helping with digestion), tomatoes, potatoes, and strawberries. Additionally, margarine, nuts/seeds, vegetable oil, and wheat germ have needed Vitamin E.

C. Additional Important Food Factors to Consider

Eating those foods that do not contain antibiotics or hormones in the growth of the meat sources is preferred for cuts of meat, fish, and fowl. (Wild salmon is preferred over farm-raised salmon, range stock preferred, etc.). This also applies to butter where organic is healthier also by most accounts.
Additionally, heavy sauces or additives to the foods for taste such as cheese, salad dressings, or gravies add calories and destroy the beneficial effects of attempts to eat healthy. (Dark apple cider vinegar and Olive Oil are preferred for salad dressing due to the fat burning properties of the vinegar and the power food benefits of the Olive Oil as already described above).

Spices and hot peppers convert food to energy while killing the bad bacteria in the stomach. They can actually act against ulcers when used in moderation.

A Harvard study identified that the 5 important helpful food categories to consider for good health were whole grains, vegetables, fruits, nuts, and yogurt for watching weight and health. (Most information states that "Greek yogurt" is preferable to others due to less additives and chemicals. Also, make sure that significant sugar content is not added to it as some do this for flavor). Those 5 most harmful food categories for weight and health include- processed meats, sugar included drinks, potato chips, white potatoes, and fatty-unprocessed meats (beef was the identified meat).

There is a lot of literature about potatoes and carbohydrates regarding a high carb diet as detrimental. Most individuals who exercise or are involved in strenuous labor activities are advised by some literature to have up to half of their daily calories come from carbohydrates as they make fuel available for the body to exert in these activities. The potato is also considered a "comfort" food as it helps produce serotonin (elevates mood) but may cause one to gain weight unless they are engaged in a highly physical work environment or routine, reoccurring exercise. (It is suggested that the typical adult gains, on average, between 3-4 pounds during their middle adult years for every 4 years). **It appears** appropriate to state that the key may be to rely on long grain rice, sweet potatoes, whole grain, or black beans (or other carb alternatives) to supply carbs when feasible. In exercise, the need for carbs to be used as fuel for exercise is essential as is it also the case, when the exercise is completed, to assist in recovery after exertion.

A breakfast that includes a hard-boiled egg and a Greek yogurt can provide up to 40%o of the daily protein requirement for some adults. Also, considering that most all animals as well as adults originated from an egg, it is reasonable to consider that the egg is a great source of practically all of the amino acids that a person's body requires daily.

A tip: Although opinions are mixed on whether pine nuts have a pleasing flavor or not (I have been given both good as well as bad reviews) they can significantly assist with weight loss. The effect of the consumed pine nuts on the stomach is that it significantly lowers the gherlin levels in the stomach. This means, essentially, that you will not have much of a hunger to prompt you to eat. The higher the level off gherlin, the more hunger so snacking on a few of these will keep your hunger at bay.

Don't Forget the Liquids-

In over 25% of those individuals with dietary issues they are also dehydrated due to lack of water in their bodies. This is a problem as we need up to an average of 8 bottled waters (or more) per day (dependent on per oz. size of the bottles).

Coffee has been shown to reduce the risk of colon cancer and some research has indicated that, drank in moderation, can assist in reducing stress and anxiety while improving mood. It is a well-known and accepted fact that caffeinated products assist in keeping of alert, yet they can be abused and become a source of addiction with detrimental results to good health.

Green Tea is very beneficial for weight control as well as for its calming effects. Green Tea has an oxidant that triggers fat release from the cells and turns this fat into energy. It also contains the amino acid theanine which has a calming effect on the brain.

4. EXERCISE-Key to elevated mood as well as improved physical functioning

Besides the obvious advantage of improving and sculpting the body muscles (as well as improving the cardiovascular system), exercise also elevates mood by initiating the firing of endorphin neurotransmitters. Heart health is improved (and the mind is sharper) due to increasing the overall neurotransmitter activity in various areas of the brain with an increase in blood flow.

The benefits include-

Elevated endorphin (neurotransmitter) firing that allow for elevated pleasure experience directly related to exercise and physical exertion.

Lower heart rate, lower blood pressure, and lower stress levels due to release of toxins through sweating and increased endorphin levels. The multiple increased neurotransmitters activity (dopamine, serotonin, endorphins) all combat anxiety, depression, and relax manic behaviors.

Choosing the Appropriate Exercise Plan- Aerobic or Anaerobic

If one is concerned primarily about cardiovascular health and flexibility they should consider aerobic exercise ("with air" exercise). This involves multiple repetitions with light weight when weight training is involved. Also, running and dance routines are a good way to aerobic exercise. You will increase stamina and muscular definition. Aerobic exercise is typically classified in three categories beginning with light (walking or house/yard work) to moderate (using the body as resistance-sit ups and pushups, chin ups, etc.), to high level as seen with Zumba and dance, stair climbers, jogging, etc. The key is that the exercise can be maintained over a continual period of time- otherwise, it becomes anaerobic. Air is used in this exercise to metabolize carbs and body fat for the workout.

If one is concerned primarily about physical strength (bulk) and gross-motor development they should consider anaerobic exercise ("without air" exercise). This is primarily using heavy weight with typically, 3 sets that regress in number of repetitions from 5 repetitions, to 3 repetitions, to 1 repetition. (When you reach 2 or more repetitions for your last set then increase weight amount for each set progressively). This routine is for increased muscle mass and increased strength. Straight carbs are the primary fuel for this form of exercise. If insufficient carbs are available in the body, then, proteins may be used from the body which means that maximum body mass development may be affected adversely.

In either event, (for anaerobic primarily) 3 days (every other day) weekly is appropriate for a muscle group and be careful to start out slow and increase gradually. Otherwise, one may "burn out" and quit exercising or experience injury due to over-exertion. Almost every exercise, in moderation, will elevate mood. The identified benefits of exercise (both physically and psychologically) include:

- Strengthens your heart and lowers blood pressure
- Increases energy levels while reducing body fat
- Strengthens and builds bones
- Improves muscle tone and strength
- Reduces stress while boosting self-esteem
- Improves sleep

- Mitigates the effects of anxiety and depressed mood

Remember: The first 4 to 6 weeks for a new exercise routine are the hardest to maintain. Once this time has past, many people are able to see the tangible results of the exercise and then it becomes easier to maintain the workout schedule. Also, the winter months are most critical for maintaining the workout schedule due to seasonal issues for depression (et. el.) and the added endorphin activity from exercise will combat those issues. And, the tendency to pack on the calories from the holiday season are addressed by diligent attention to the workout schedule during the winter months.

Note: Some exercise and nutritional experts suggest that you drink an 8 oz. glass of milk (some specify chocolate milk) after a workout to aid in recovery and de-stress of the body. If one is planning on eating a meal with carbohydrates within 1 to 1 ½ hours after a workout, then the milk is not necessary, they conclude.

5. A STRUCTURED DAILY SCHEDULE

A structured daily schedule includes eating, sleeping, exercising, having leisure time, working (or having a purpose/hobby that is motivating and challenging), exploring personal spiritual development, and time for meditation or reflection on your life will assist in the optimal opportunity for good mental health.

Traditionally, work allows one to fulfill their financial needs, elevate their self-esteem due to being self-reliant, and keep their day occupied without time to ruminate or allow excess time that leads to practicing poor mental health (addiction, dysfunctional thinking/behaviors, etc.)

Work is something that can be a source of challenge or dread. It is important to be happy with what one is doing to maximize their positive mental health experiences from work. One must consider that since close to a third of their overall day (and up to half or more of their waking time daily) is spent in work for a great deal of their adult life-they should approach it in a manner that allows them to maximize their benefits and positive experiences from work.

NOTE* - I encourage clients to understand that all jobs are important- or, they would not exist. This thought is offered in reference to clients having a poor opinion of a job they hold. just keep working appreciating your efforts in the interim. towards gaining the optimal position while gaining skills for their dream job.

6. **WORK- Development of Knowledge, Skills, and Abilities and the Process of Finding the Career "Perfect" Job Match**

A common tool used to determine the fitness of a person for a particular job and, likewise, the fitness of the job for a particular person, is to use an **interest inventory survey** ["Strong Interest Inventory" is a reputable test measure]. This is available for anyone by a search on the internet and will result in availability for an often, nominal fee for the person to take the survey. This survey will match your interests and job preferences as well as your life goals with the jobs that your skills and abilities are best suited for.

One of the concepts behind the use of an interest inventory is that the goal is to match the personality type (realistic, investigative, social, enterprising, artistic, or conventional- from John Holland, 1997) of the individual against the factors important to a career. The individual's actual tendencies regarding various skills needed for a particular general type of job (mechanical, administrative, social, and analytical, etc.) are considered in completing an analysis of the person. These (and other) factors associated with the person-in comparison to those needed knowledge, skills, and abilities for the job- are weighed. The goal is to match the person while taking into consideration what they like doing, in complement to what the necessary job skills for the job. The goal is, in the end, to find what the person is best suited to excel in and enjoy doing.

Briefly considered, the work-related personality types are explained as follows:

- Realistic- deal with environment in an objective, concrete, and physically manipulate their work (with their hands). Prefer agricultural, technical, skilled trades, and engineering work. Examples of jobs include motor skills, equipment/machine work and working with tools.

- Investigative- deal with environment by use of their intellect-use symbolism such as language, art, words, and ideas. They prefer scientific vocations or work with art, music, and sculpture. They achieve academically and usually make poor leaders.

- Social- use social skills and thrive off of social interactions. They prefer educational, therapeutic, or religious vocations and activities. They view themselves as conservative, responsible, self-accepting.

- Enterprising- cope with their environment by adventurous, dominant, enthusiastic, or impulsive qualities. They are typically persuasive and verbally skilled as well as extroverted. They can be aggressive and excel in sales, supervisory, and leadership roles.

- Artistic- they usually create art forms and products to interact with their environment. They are subjective and utilize fantasy to express themselves.

They function best in musical, artistic, literary, and dramatic vocations that are creative based.

- Conventional- they are goal-oriented and need social approval. They are both sociable yet conservative while being standard/conventional in their approach to problem-solving. Clerical, accounting, business, and economist roles are best suited vocations with mathematical skills as assets they possess.

Once this initial task has been accomplished and the person makes a decision as to what they lifetime ambition is employment wise-make a plan to get the job. When working at any job ask yourself- "How is this job gaining me the skills that I need to be able to get the dream job that I ultimately want?" Every job should be a stepping stone to lead the person to achieve their employment goals. If it is not, I suggest that one should be looking to do so as is possible.

I have found it necessary to expend, often, limited resources to get a resume and cover letter that highlights fitness for employment with a realistic sales pitch to gain you the opportunity for an interview. Then you can attempt to convince the interviewer that you are someone that they just "have to have" for their company. Being happy at work is also a benefit to good mental health.

Remember- a job is a real possession and if the job was not important then it would not exist. Be pleased to possess it.

7. HAVING A SPIRITUAL EXISTENCE- A Bedrock to Developing a Relationship with our Source and Coping Skills for Life

An understanding must be made- religion is the established set of rituals, with a building, and social association for like-minded people to congregate for worship.

On the other hand, spirituality is the individual, personal development of a relationship between yourself and the One whom you perceive as your Source. The coping and support that one receives from having a basic, spiritual existence cannot be underestimated as it allows one to cope with life.

They have the belief that someone is looking out for them, they have something into the future to anticipate that is typically viewed as good, and conversely, if things do not go well in this moment it does not mean that they should just "give up". In short, it allows for a wonderful virtue to exist in their life- HOPE.

This is truly a worthwhile personal journey that I would recommend for anyone as a means of making sense and having peace in a world that may frequently be hard to accept while being frustrated during our lifetime. This is a major source for your meditation time and serves as the topic for personal reflection and inquiry. Common questions of spiritual nature include our meaning and purpose for life. The benefits include lower suicide rates, longer life due to healthier behaviors, and more prosocial attitudes and behaviors. Themes of humility, caring and empathy, love for self and others, patience, and service to others often result from a spiritual existence that takes time daily for prayer and meditation.

Understand, our development has both critical periods for learning as well as sensitive periods for learning-essentially, some things have to be mastered at specific moments (critical periods) while other things may be mastered at various times but not only one moment (sensitive periods). (Many people ensure that spiritual experiences are available to their early childhood family member to instill spiritual qualities to their thinking).

A critical period mastery involves spiritual intelligence. (The idea that we learn spiritual concepts and they become our foundation from which we address problems and crisis moments). The values and moral compass will serve as their way to respond to life's challenges and without a spiritually oriented early learning format-something will take its place as our foundation of our moral fiber. My research has shown me that hedonism and materialism have a better chance of being important when this early-childhood, and subsequent, spiritual experience is lacking.

Example: The "Golden Rule" teaches one to treat others the way that they wish to be treated. An absence of this knowledge may lead someone to act in their own best interest (rather than in another's best interests). This may be the preferred manner of behavior without spiritual intelligence.

Finally, as this writer has done research for writing of books on spirituality, I have found various explanations for what is spiritual, what is a spiritual life, and what does it consist of. One of the best explanations that I read during researching was that **we need to be positively connected on 3 levels** order to be realizing a satisfying and compelling spiritual life. The idea was that one need be connected positively to (1) **our Source**, our (2) **fellow human**, and (3) **our environment (nature).** This is a goal to work towards to gain a sense of spiritual mastery in your life.

8. A LEISURE LIFESTYLE- The Final Part to the Puzzle of Daily Practices for Good Mental Health

In close to 90% of the instances when Behavioral Activation was used in the treatment of depression, positive results were achieved with a great reduction or elimination of depressed mood for the patient in treatment.

Simply put, people talk about what they are interested in or are doing in their daily lives. If one is recreating on a daily or regular basis they will be either talking about what they are going to do, are doing, or did for recreation. It is reasonable to assume that their positive experience from recreation will be more advantageous than the negative mental health experience that they are otherwise experiencing. This adds up to a great deal of time that is in opposition to emotional pain associated with poor, personal mental health experiences.

Behavioral Activation involves planning a daily, 1+ hour per activity, that includes others (not solitary activities), and allows for journaling before and after the event. Choosing previously enjoyable activities from their lives are used to schedule a calendar for themselves and those in their life on a reoccurring, routine basis. For best results a minimum of 4-5 days a week/weekend should have events.

Advantages to Behavioral Activation- A Leisure Lifestyle

Recreational therapist plan events that include 4 components whenever possible as part of the recreational outing. They are-social, physical, cognitive, and emotional. I have found that spiritual-based activities are also necessary.

Solitary events are not beneficial except for when time to reflect or relax require them (meditation and spiritual-oriented reflection). However, avoid using that as an explanation for preference for solitary events. Social associations and connection to others allow for forming and developing relationships. They help to keep people connected with their friends, family, and community.

Physical (gross or fine motor skill use) and cognitive (memory- both procedural and declarative) components allow for fighting the effects of aging and mental health issues that typically affect those aspects negatively.
Final analysis is that leisure activities improve functioning and elevate mood.
Identified benefits for a leisure lifestyle include:

- Decrease in depressive symptoms
- Elevated emotional well-being
- Increased independence, self-esteem, and confidence
- Increased motivation, improved quality of life, and reduced isolation.
- Strengthened mental well-being
- Promotes community integration
- Reduces stress and anxiety

Setting up a Behavioral Activation Plan
REALIZING GOOD MOOD AND FUNCTIONING

WRITE a list of at least 12-15 different recreational activities that you have enjoyed in your life. They must include people and have a duration of in excess of 1 hour each. Schedule each of these activities into a calendar that is typically at minimum of 4 to 5 activities for each week (this will be a 3 week schedule when you are done).

JOURNAL for each activity-before, grade from "1" (bad) to "10" (awesome) the expected experience for the upcoming activity just prior to the event. Also, discuss what you expect will happen, what you would like to have happen, etc.

THEN- Enjoy the activity with others (social events are great ways to build relationships). Journal after the activity-what happened, grade it 1-10, and discuss what happened and if you would do it again, what other events could be done in the future, who you met, etc. At the end of the 3 weeks, schedule the top 5-7 events on a routine, reoccurring calendar with exceptions to keep the calendar fresh and not become stale.

IN SUMMARY-MANAGING OUR EMOTIONAL STATE FOR GOOD MENTAL HEALTH

Having a good mental health state requires us to be able to function well physically, mentally, emotionally, and spiritually-free of distress.
Being free of distress is wishful thinking as life continues to throw curves at us. This being the case, we need to relieve ourselves of as much stress as is possible so that the distress does not overtake us and render us ineffective in dealing with excessive mental health issues. Common thinking in therapy is that more than 3 stressors ongoing constitutes a dangerous situation to function within.

Although thinking, feeling, and behaviors are important to realizing good mental health-the daily grind and typical aspects of life such as work, play, and rest are also vital to good functioning.
We must control our environment rather than have it control us-taking care of the little things and self-care will allow us to weather storms that will undoubtedly occur in spite of our best efforts. The final key to good emotional (and all other aspects of functioning) is to have a reason for your life that you have identified and are motivated and engaged in bringing to a successful conclusion. In short-

HAVE A PURPOSE TO YOUR LIFE- (See Worksheet 2 **(WK 4)** at the back of the book for guidance in tackling this activity).

It seems safe to assume that people will not get in their cars and begin driving without having somewhere in mind. Wouldn't make much sense or so it seems. So, why would one go through life without a plan to make full use of their resources in order to achieve the most from life. In short, we need a plan for life.

A common occurrence that I observe is that there are some people who do not have enough hours in the day, whereas, there are others who use distractions to fill their waking hours. If you have something that is really important to your life and supplies the description of how you lived your "dash", then pursue it. Doing so will keep you busy so that you can avoid falling into the traps of substance as well as other mental health problems.

Start by determining what your "purpose for living" is, then **make a "plan"** to achieve that purpose. Your plan will be **made up of "goals"** and each goal will **require that certain "steps" be accomplished**. These steps require **your time daily to complete "tasks"** so that the **steps will be completed**, the **goals** will be **reached**, and your **plan is finalized to fulfill your purpose** realized upon entering the final stage of your developmental cycle that considers your life's work. Your time will be well-used and you will feel a sense of accomplishment when you consider your life. **The purpose is to live a life well-spent.**

(4-A)

CORE AREA 4- Implementing Change to Improve Life

<u>Suggested Recommendations</u>

1. Consult with a dietary specialist to design a daily food diet based on caloric needs, energy needs for exercise programming, and with consideration for metabolism from thyroid activity & physical exertion

2. Schedule a leisure lifestyle calendar that addresses spiritual, cognitive, physical, social, and emotional needs. Activities need the involvement of others- not sedentary/isolating activities. Build relationships based on healthy living.

3. Practice breathing and relaxation techniques as appropriate and needed to address stress, anxiety, and panic symptoms.

4. Work with a physical trainer to design an exercise program that addresses the goals you find important- e.g. flexibility (stretching and yoga), strength (anaerobic), stamina (aerobic), and endurance (cross-training).

5. Develop a personal, fulfilling spiritual basis for living which supports and develops your belief system. The practices should allow for personal growth that supports the practitioner in meaningful ways to be there for them (especially when they are in extremely stressful or life changing situations).

6. Make a plan for your life. Short-term, medium-range, and long-term goals that support a lifetime purpose for living is an essential part of planning. (A worksheet is available at the back of this manual for your consideration).

7. Set up time each day to have communications (and shared time) with your spouse, children, and those you believe are important. (Some estimates are that parents typically spend less than 15 minutes talking with their kids daily. Do not neglect your relationships so that misunderstandings may develop, or children do not have access to your knowledge.

CORE AREA FIVE
IT'S ALL ABOUT COPING-
Failure to cope is at the root of poor behaviors and ineffective coping allows for poor mental health

INTRODUCTION- It is reasonable to assume that people do things because they see a benefit for themselves (or others) by doing/not doing whatever it is that is under consideration at the time. Their thinking that there is an advantage may not be true or accurate, but their judgment sees it as a benefit. They may also see their thinking to be normal, right, or appropriate. This thinking (as has been discussed in the "thinking" (CBT- Core area 1) may be irrational or destructive to their best interests, nevertheless, they engage in those thinking processes and, from them, they try to cope with life (or react to life) with formulas such as: EITHER WORRY, FEELING DEPRESSED, OR EXHIBIT MANIC BEHAVIORS AS A RESPONSE TO THEIR ENVIRONMENT OR LIFE SITUATION.

MENTAL HEALTH DISORDERS AS COPING METHODS

A REASONABLE QUESTION IS- "What are you getting out of it that you find productive?" (If not-why do you continue to use those methods for coping?)

Worry, avoidance, self-medicating behaviors, (and other mental disordered symptoms), are not coping methods although those who utilize them appear to believe from their early life experience that they are useful. Their awareness, acceptance, and application of these practices suggest a perceived benefit or usefulness to doing so- if only unintentionally, or, in a subconscious way. It becomes a basis for "normal" (Core Area 6).

PRIMARY LEVEL OF INEFFECTIVE COPING- Making the point

Initially, mental health concerns begin with the child in the environment. Anxiety, depression, bipolar, and psychosis have been determined to have some origins in genetics (not a total explanation, environment is important also). The child has access to behaviors and practices in their environment that may directly, or indirectly, affect their mental health. Adding to this, the genetic effect as well, the primary level of dysfunction can occur.

SECONDARY LEVEL OF INEFFECTIVE COPING

People use means and methods to cope so that they will either not feel bad or feel better. Additionally, they may do so because they believe that their coping method will lead to accomplishing what they want (or feel is right to do).

When they do so they employ resources or practice different behaviors to accomplish the resolution to their stressors or problems. Some of the means or resources include- drugs, alcohol, distractions, work, food, sex, are often used rather than actually dealing with the stress, loss, or problems. (This is because of the societal rules that suggests, "If you feel bad, take a pill, then you will feel good (an emotion)" and "you must be happy, or doing something to be happy" (dysfunctional thinking).

Please Note* - **When happiness is the sole ambition or avoiding taking care of problems, (acting without rational-based thinking to problem-solve), you are you not effectively dealing with the issues. You are often adding additional problems, forming additional mental health related symptoms, and causing stress-related illnesses.**

A TERTIARY (3ᴿᴰ) LEVEL OF MENTAL HEALTH DYSFUNCTION

When people employ worry, a depressed mood, or manic presentation-they develop other behaviors that lead to additional mental health disorders. Often, due to underdeveloped ego integrity they develop personality disorders. Personality disorders result when dysfunctional thinking is used to form beliefs regarding them self and their self within their environment that are unhealthy. They are ineffectively ways to view their life. These disorders cause problems that add additional mental health diagnoses to understanding their lives.

The idea is that the much of personality develops beginning with the end of egocentric behaviors (around age 11) onward to the time of the matured adult ego (some estimate the age of 21 to 24 for adult ego solidification). When the person has damaging personality issues such as those listed below, they fail to develop optimally and have additional problems to overcome. (Some research indicates that over 70% of substance abusers have personality disorders also).

(Personality disorders do not usually disappear but often may diminish and wane with many people as they progress into later adulthood).

The below categories are explanations of personality-related, dysfunctional symptoms of behavior. Many, or most, people can identify with having had these symptoms but, only when they significantly impair the person's daily lifestyle, is a potential diagnosis merited.

Some of the issues associated with and serve as a basis for the development of personality-related disorders include: Themes of disconnect and rejection, impaired independence and performance, impaired personal limits, other-directedness, and over-vigilance and inhibition. The below are examples of how these themes are perceived by the under-developed, ego.

Personality disorders as dysfunctional coping styles- the developmental schemas during their adolescent origins. *(The following categories and information are from "Cognitive Behavior Therapy for Personality Disorders" by Len Sperry).*

General category of disconnection and rejection.....................................
Abandonment and instability-others will not or cannot provide reliable and stable support.
Mistrust/abuse-others will abuse, humiliate, cheat, lie, manipulate, or take advantage of them.
Defectiveness/shame- one is ineffective, bad, unwanted, or inferior to others.
Social isolation/alienation-one is alienated, different from others, or not part of a group.

General category of impaired autonomy and performance...........................

Dependence/incompetence-belief that one is unable to fulfill their everyday responsibilities without others having a significant impact or taking charge.
Vulnerability to harm/illness- excessive fear of catastrophe and of personal inability to deal with those situations.
Enmeshment/underdeveloped self- the belief in close attachment over independence and personal development.
Failure- belief that one will inevitably fail or is fundamentally inadequate to deal with life's challenges consistently.

General category of impaired limits...

Entitlement/grandiosity-One thinks that they are superior to others and that the rules don't apply to them.
Lack of self-control, self-discipline, and effective self-monitoring-the presence of low frustration-tolerance and attending to fewer cues to arrive at actions.

General category of other-directedness...

Subjugation-placing the needs, desires, and feelings of others above their own in order to be liked, avoid criticism, or retaliation.
Self-sacrifice- belief that others gratification is more important than fulfilling their own needs.
Approval-seeking/recognition-seeking- constant seeking belonging or acceptance from others rather than developing personal character and achieving self-actualization and personal ambitions.

General category of over-vigilance and inhibition...

Negativity/pessimism- a pervasive, lifelong focus on the negative aspects of life while minimizing the positive and optimistic possibilities.

Emotional inhibition- avoidance of spontaneous emotions and behaviors or expression because of fear of disapproval, shame, or losing personal control.

Unrelenting standards/hyper-criticalness- an unrealistically high expectations and goals for conduct or performance.

These thinking and behavior patterns are learned and developed primarily in adolescence and follow the person into adulthood with personality disorders that represent additional mental health diagnoses from ineffective coping.

Mental health dysfunction via ineffective coping either from the personality-related issues or from their dysfunctional perceived "normal" within their environment:

Summary to this point..
Anxiety, depression, or mania (and other mental health related disorders) result from dysfunctional thinking that equates their use for coping to deal with their lives when their lives appears difficult or impossible.

Development of personality disorders, as a result of dysfunctional schema that develop during adolescent or early adulthood, have a component associated with their development of ineffective coping or isolation. (Those who abuse substances, develop addictions, have other mental health issues often are prone to this form of mental health dysfunctional formation).

Since they must deceive or hide their substance use, gain habits or patterns of behavior to address those dysfunctional personality concerns, or otherwise avoid the tasks associated with development of mature behavior-they may end with mental health issues. Primarily this results from ineffective coping skills.

Modeled behaviors and bad life experience ferments and builds the dysfunction until it becomes problematic. Further, ineffective thinking when loss, physical pain, stress, or grief occurs also adds fuel to this development. The failure to consider positive or beneficial approach to tragedy serve as an additional theme for dysfunction. Finally, inaccurate yet derogatory "facts" about self help promote dysfunction.

Examples of ineffective thinking leading to coping catastrophizing

The loss of a loved one..

Was the person in pain or had lived a long life? If so, are they better in a different place absent pain-or-are you concerned with your own loss and the dependence on their being in your life vs. being more concerned about taking personal responsibility for your own happiness?

A common phrase is that "everything happens for a reason". This seems appropriate and our lack of understanding does not mean that a reason does not exist-only that we don't know what the reason (or reasoning) is.

Instead, we see the loss as what we have lost-the person who is gone fails to be the focus in such an instance. Having a primary interest in self over others is often seen as "selfish" by some.

Other examples of catastrophizing coping in action (One of the most common sources of anxiety and depression)

A lack of money, physical pain, or a personally demeaning status such as lack of personal residence for living ....

If we don't have enough money we do have a safety net called social services-problem is that this brings up an additional thinking dysfunction- pride (feeling- an emotion) and how we feel about receiving the aid. Physical pain may be debilitating, yet, sound healthcare practices (pain management) can somewhat mitigate the severity.

If we have **a potential loss of residence**......again, there are resources- we can't allow our pride (feeling- an emotion) to deter us from a sensible consideration of our situation. **If we haven't achieved as we had dreamed of to that point**- we still have the remainder of our lives to do so (or do you prefer to be anxious and depressed?) Sound healthcare places the responsibility back on the person from a rational-based perspective. **Remember, sometimes emotions are all that we have at the moment, but, we need to refocus as soon as we can to resolve the pain.**

A common issue for those with substance abuse or mental health issues involves the feeling, early in recovery, that they have ruined their lives and they have no future...

People need to understand that they review their life for its success (or failure) when the life span has been complete. When we do not give ourselves the opportunity to view our complete life at its fullest extent, we fail to realize our potential. I find that many recovering addicts bemoan their failures and mistakes without realizing that, as long as they learned valuable lessons from those situations, they were not failure but learning experiences that will allow them to reach their ambitions as long as they continue to stand up. Success is only possible when we stand up one more time than we fell down.

Beyond changing our perspectives when addressing coping nightmares, the general need to think more appropriately when we face problems encourages us to utilize a basic, routine way to deal with challenges and stressor daily.

We need to have a simplified, expedient way to make decisions to deal with what is thrown at us. **This is essential to best utilize our most precious resource ...our ...time.**

THE GOAL: We need to have basic problem-solving skills and a consistent strategy to ensure we are ahead of the curve. We should aim at being proactive in our life-rather than being reactive and always trying to "CATCH UP" when we face adversity.

THE I.D.E.A.L. PROBLEM-SOLVING METHOD

Around the end of the 1980s, with further publication in the early 1990's, Bransford and Stein introduced a strategy for problem-solving that was both simple- yet effective. This strategy was devised as a way initially to help inner-city youths to deal with problems by way of a problem-solving strategy with the goal of allow their youths to achieve improved functioning while avoiding problem behaviors that were detrimental to their development. This simple, problem-solving strategy was known by the acronym of I.D.E.A.L. which stands for ... "I" (IDENTIFY THE PROBLEM), "D" (DETERMINE THE ISSUES), "E" (EVALUATE THE OPTIONS/CHOICES), "A" (ACT), AND "L" (LEARN).

(I am not using the method in its form yet the acronym of IDEAL to add ease to learning). Although this seems simple there is some thought that is involved to master this step-by-step manner of handling life's problems. Before going into the details of the method, a brief consideration of issues associated with problem-solving are now discussed.

Considerations as one approaches problem-solving

Terms to understand...

Problem perspective-the initial point when one is aware that there is a problem or issue that needs to be dealt with.

Problem self-efficacy-how one feels about their ability to handle problems (both too low or too high are detrimental to effectively resolve problems).

Problem orientation-the manner in which someone approaches a problem (perspective and preferences for proceeding forward in resolution- totally or in parts, as a team member or individualist, at ease or nervous, forward to back or from back to front, etc.)

Problem format-this follows the problem orientation stage and is basically how we express the problem to self and others when explaining the problem. If we do not express the problem accurately-it will be hard to break it down into parts and resolve it. Further, you must consider "lateral thinking" as a part of this format exercise.

Lateral thinking-when expressing the problem, we may choose to look at the problem in a broader context or in a narrower way of explaining the problem (its size, content, or who is involved) so that we can format in a way that is both accurate and makes the problem easier to arrive at a solution.

A need to consider the concept of self-efficacy- the belief in the ability of self to be able to do things and at what level of competence we feel we are operating at. Compare these:

Low self-efficacy is the belief that we cannot handle situations and will invariably fail. When we function in this state our lives easily become unmanageable. (Tendency for procrastination).

High self-efficacy is the belief that we will not fail and will overcome any challenges (they are not seen as problems). The only thing to beware of is that failure is inevitable, and one need be cautious to not let this disappointment lead to doubting self. We are human, only do our best and do not quit. (Tendency to be impulsive).

Positive/adaptive problem orientation includes-
The ability to recognize a problem accurately when it occurs.
The belief that problems are normal and inevitable part of life.
The ability to identify or attribute the "cause" of the problem accurately.
The tendency to appraise new problems as "challenges" rather than as "catastrophes" or situations to be avoided.
The desire to solve the problem in a timely manner.
The ability to inhibit the tendency to be impulsive when solving stressful problems or issues.

Important considerations to be effective in problem-solving:
Seek important facts and information concerning the problem.
Describe the facts in a clear and unambiguous manner and concisely.
Differentiate objective facts from unverified information, assumptions, or interpretations.
Identify the factors and circumstances that make the situation a problem, and-
Set a series of realistic problem-solving goals.

Individual's ability to resolve problems

Experts-see the finer points and all aspects of the issue where novice problem-solving is associated with a general, overall solution that may need to be fine-tuned for a specific situation or event.

Declarative knowledge (general knowledge of facts and information) that is a basis for the process of problem-solving, and,

Procedural knowledge (steps and processes knowledge of how to do something) that serves the basis of process to accomplish a solution to the problem.

Associated skills (administrative) and analogical (past experience in similar situations) are also valuable to the problem-solving skill development for the individual.

For novel problem-solving situations some solution skills include:

Reproductive problem-solving involves replicating the events and processes that led to the problem to find out where things went wrong and how to fix the issue.

Means-end analysis is the process of breaking down into all of the parts to see which part is causing the issue- then, working to fix that part.

Productive thinking- this is using a decision tree (if this, then that will happen, etc.)

Cost/Benefit Analysis- the pros versus the cons and whether the good out weights the bad, or, if that which is good is superior to the bad.

Analogous Problem Solving- "this is what happened last time and it is happening again in the same manner, so we will fix it this way again" (example). The biggest consideration is that one must have a direct "transfer of knowledge" that supports that the situations are the same in actuality-this is essential for this strategy to work. Often times, the fact that time has past since the last instance serves to guarantee that the situation is not identical in meaningful ways.

Flexibility and patience are essential for any of these methods to work. These ways are quick approaches to problem-solving but a consistent manner that can be routinely used to handle a wide array of issues is the IDEAL method which, when used consistently, will also develops critical-thinking skills! See below:

THE IDEAL PROBLEM-SOLVING METHOD
(THE STEPS AND CONSIDERATIONS)

Note* - Each letter spelling IDEAL is a step in the process/5 letters = 5 steps. (See Worksheet 5 **(WK 5)** for an outline and sheet to practice this method).

Step #1- Identifying the problem

This may be the hardest part of the process as there are times when what has happened previous to the event (earlier in the day, week, year, or even earlier) are the cause for our anger or stress.

There may be more than one problem to consider-if so, which one needs to be dealt with first, or, does the problem really even need to be directly addressed?

Will the problem lead to another situation if resolved? If so, what and is it better to table the issue until a more permanent solution can be devised to handle everything?

Is the problem yourself? Is it not a problem and only you are angry or negatively affected?

Step #2 – Determin(e)ing the issues

The easiest way to use this step is to ask yourself the question of "who, what, where, when, why, and how". If you can answer each of these parts to analyze and determine the problem, then you will tend to settle on understanding what specifically is at stake and where there are issues.

Another reasonable question to ask is "who are the stakeholders in the problem?" this is important to determine who has to be taken into account when a decision is reached. People matter and a prosocial approach to problem-solving requires all parties to be respected, secured, and considered.

Step #3- Evaluat(e)ing the options

Does the option resolve the problem totally or is something else (or additional steps) required to completely resolve all of the issues of the problem?

Ensure that no one is detrimentally affected by the options or choices you lean towards as a solution.

Is it efficient? You don't spend $10 dollars to handle a .05 (cent) problem.

What is the best option among those available?

Are you satisfied with the expected results or is more to be considered? (Go back to step 1 and go forward with each different issue as is appropriate and in a timely manner).

Step #4 – Act

Seemingly simple as a step, knowing when to act is just important as doing so in a productive, effective, and cost-conscious manner.

Sometimes it is best to allow someone the opportunity to correct the issues rather than always take charge-however, have an option available to use if it becomes important and necessary to act.

Don't hurt others unless it is not possible to avoid doing so-and-only if they are the proximal cause of the problem. Regardless, be considerate that they may be expected to tender the same regard for you in the future- "Don't cause yourself future problems" is a reasonable consideration.

Always have a plan in place to abort the actions if necessary.

Step #5 - Learn

An old adage is that there is never failure when one learns from a mistake. Keep this in mind and avoid thinking that once solved, it is the end of it. For everything that is resolved there is a follow-up (cause-and-effect in operation).

Military protocol is to have a "debriefing" after every exercise, action, or operation. Consider this process (learning) an opportunity to debrief yourself and those involved in the problem so that all can learn different, better, more effective, etc. ways to handle similar situations in the future.

Allow this process to give you confidence and elevate your self-esteem as you demonstrate competence in dealing with life. This is preferred to experiencing situations of anxiety, depression, mania, or dysfunctional personality related behaviors due to irrational thinking as has been described.

Coping- Additional Considerations and Options

When is it better to "let a sleeping dog lie"? Ask yourself whether it will or will not matter in say, 5 years- if not, don't stress is usually the best policy. Not everything needs to be solved and some problems do need to be ignored. The real skill is in being able to realize what is important and needs attention and what is better left alone.

Consider thought-attacking or thought-blocking strategies instead.

Thought-attacking and thought-blocking strategies are available to address such things and to allow one to avoid the anxiety and depressed state traps that continued "ruminating behavior"(over-and-over stressing about something) allows.

An example I use to describe "ruminating behavior" is to ask one to consider the blue circle that continually goes around and around on their computer screen when it is "rebooting". When it fails to stop then-that is "ruminating". Most mental disorders have this as a central feature for the person who suffers from them. (They are problematic both during waking hours or when attempting to fall off to sleep).

Thought blocking strategies- (See Worksheet 4 **(WK 6)** for help with this concept at the back of the book).

They are very simple and basically consist of ways to distract oneself away from the ruminating behaviors such as – "naming the roster for the 1972 Washington Redskins football team" (an example), or, what were the names of your friends in elementary school? (Or, who were the teachers then?).
The idea is to concentrate on something that requires your full, undivided attention and does not allow you to focus on the ruminating thoughts.
Other examples including counting backwards from 1,000 by 7's –or- count backwards in the alphabet from "z" by every 4th letter. (That is the really hard one that will guarantee to get you to forget the ruminating thought(s)). You may devise one of your own by deeply considering your interest (e.g. If like books, then, "What are your ten favorite and why, what author is your favorite and why, etc." You get the idea)? Just choose whatever is your interest and mentally consider your interests with questions such as why, what, when, where, how, etc. regarding your areas of interest.

Thought-attacking strategies- (See Worksheet 3 **(WK 7)** for help with this concept at the back of the book).

There is a simple one that I have found that works that was considered a therapy strategy by some clinicians some time ago. It seems better considered as a thought-attacking strategy instead. The strategy, as I address it, comes from "the work of Byron Katie".

I have closely presented it below as a means of attacking the thoughts as they relate to rumination for the anxious and depressed individual. They are, in order;

   (1) Is what you are ruminating actually true?
   (2) Then, is it true beyond a shadow of a doubt?
   (3) If so- consider your physical, emotional, and mental state as a result of the knowledge that the ruminating thought is reality. Be in touch with yourself and, finally,
   (4) Take the physical, emotional, mental state and adjust it so that it is healthy by adjusting your thinking to a more positive, optimistic perspective-

Do this by asking yourself ways that the "problem" has a "silver lining" and the glass is "half full" (rather than "half empty") **(Thinking Approach)** or use the

Breathing/Progressive Relaxation strategy found in Core Area 4 **(Physcial Approach).**

A scriptural adage tells us that what is good, holy, right, or pleasing-think on these things and there is a certain truth to understand from this verse. It is at the core of thought attacking as a technique.

SUMMARY

Mental health disorders such as depression of anxiety (mainly worry) can be ill-advised means that people use to cope with life. Poor coping also leads to further mental health problems such as addiction and personality disorders (as well as allow those disorder to continue and progress is severity). This, in turn, leads to further elevation to the initial mental health issues. It is a vicious circle.

Problem-solving strategies offer an opportunity to effectively address life issues while helping the self-esteem and self-concept of the person. This results in the person feeling like they are able to manage their lives with elevated self-efficacy (what the person thinks of their abilities to do a particular thing). Critical-thinking skills are improved and strengthened by using these problem-solving methods thereby making the person better prepared to tackle life Learning what tool to use and when is at the basis of effective functioning to deal with life in a positive, prosocial, and healthy manner to avert the stress and pain of ineffective coping strategies.

(5-A)

CORE AREA 5- Questions for Consideration

1. If you worry or are depressed over something does it make the thing or situation better?

2. If you don't worry or are not depressed over something does it guarantee that the thing or situation will be better?

3. If you answered "no" to both questions, then;

WHICH IS BETTER FOR YOUR MENTAL HEALTH AS A WAY OF BEHAVING AND THINKING? (Worry, or, Resolving the Problem)?

4. If you DID NOT ANSWER "NO" TO BOTH QUESTIONS, why do you believe that either of these two questions should be answered "YES"?

5. What is actually going to take care of the stressor or problem? Avoidance, denial, ignoring, or dealing with what is the issue?

6. Is just being happy ensure that stressors or problems are resolved?

CORE AREA SIX
The 40/40/20 Developmental Progression-
How We Get to Where We Are and From Where We Get Those Dysfunctional Ideas and Behaviors

Introduction to the 40/40/20 Model

It has been theorized that we learn and develop 40% of who and what we are from our parents and siblings, we learn and develop 40% of who and what we are from our peers, coworkers, and colleagues, and the final 20% of who and what we are (and become) is based on how we interpret our world and all of our life experiences.

There are different developmental stage models that address various aspects of our growth and development- they include a moral development model (Kohlberg), reasoning and deduction model (Piaget), a developmental stage model for the person (Erickson), and systems thinking from family therapy that addresses the various systems operating for each person (family, friends, community, region, nation, civilization, etc.).

A Precursor to Understanding the Developmental Models-

The parenting we receive (or don't receive), as well as how we relate to our initial relationships (mother, father, or guardian) has a great impact on how well we grow and mature as an individual. Relating to our earliest relationships involves attachment (research considers "attachment theory"). I will first consider these two issues (parenting styles and attachment theory) briefly to lead into a discussion of the various models describing our maturity process.

PARENTING STYLES- (The environment in which the child lives within).

When acting in a parenting style to assist your child to develop, know that the temperament of the child should be considered in determining the specific parenting responses. However, the various, traditionally identified parenting styles (not responses to specific situations) include:

Authoritative- This parenting style is both demanding of development towards becoming a mature, responsible adult while being responsive to the child's needs. Mature development includes demonstrating positive problem-solving behaviors and allows for progressively expanded independence and self-reliance for decision-making. The parent monitors and guides the child and allows the child to approach them free of embarrassment or ridicule to discuss issues that are often sensitive. Punishment is consistently administered, and the child is provided the reasons for the punishment as well as discussing the need for improvements. Providing understanding as to what the ramifications could be for those poor behaviors becomes important. Positive encouragement is also important and carefully balanced to show support and awareness of prosocial behaviors as well as those needing improvement.

This method of parenting has consistently been shown to provide the best long-term results for the child as they enter adulthood.

Authoritarian- This is heavily punishment-laden, style that fails to consistently address behaviors of the child in order to provide explanations or guidance. Behaviors are expected with little discussion or consideration for the status of the child in the family structure. ("Don't do as I do, do as I say do" parental attitude). It seems appropriate to consider that this style is not necessarily based on bad intentions and is designed to teach the child to operate in a hostile, harsh environment that they may encounter in adulthood ("toughen them up" mentality). However, the child is often less socially-competent, and this parenting style may stunt long-term, positive, growth. The child is prone to rebel in adolescence although they typically are conformist and socially obedient (yet often unhappy) as adults.

Indulgent/Permissive- The goal of the parent is, in actual results, to be a "friend" to their child and behavioral expectations are few and inconsistently expected. Although the parent is heavily involved in the child's life (taking the child to sports, music and dance lessons, events, etc.)-the role of teacher and guidance for the child is lacking with little discipline demonstrated. It is not uncommon to hear the indulgent parent state that "they want to give the child what they never had" (without providing the guidance and monitoring that goes with the development process for the child). (Note: Narcissistic personality related issues are estimated to be found in over 25% of individuals aged 18 to 30- and "entitled" mindset is prevalent in these instances. It appears reasonable that, this parenting style has a major impact negatively towards these issues).

Neglectful- Although the parent may be able to provide, or be providing a home and food, there is little or no personal warmth and support/guidance for the child. Even worse, the absence of the basic necessities may be present without stable support for the child. Without the trust gained from having support and a demonstrated interest in the child's maturity and quality of life, the child is at risk to not develop appropriately-either emotionally or socially. Without the trust gained from having support, the child may have great difficulty navigating thru the various lessons to be learned and experiences to be gained towards positive personal growth. This parenting style benefits from education and social support from the community and experienced family members. The parents can learn to provide stable and responsible parenting experiences for their children thru this education so that society is at less risk from delinquency.

ATTACHMENT THEORY- (Developing Trust & Inquiring Minds Towards Their Environment).

Not only is parenting essential as a means of understanding how the child approaches the following developmental models, how the child initially (and subsequently) interacts with their caregivers is important. Theory of attachment (Ainsworth and Bowlby) suggest that how we learn to attach as infants and early children will affect how we attach to others as adults. Essentially, the infant needs to feel secure and have a safe haven while they learn about their environment. They may either have a **secure, an insecure (2 types), or disorganized attachment style** towards their caregiver. The literature points to 4 basic possibilities which are:

#1- Secure Attachment- The infant feels safe and knows that, when uncertainty or problems related to dealing with their immediate environment occur-they have a safe place (caregiver) to fall back on. The caregiver is perceived by the infant to be available, will be there when needed, and treats the infant "well". This allows the infant to develop with a progression forward to more and more complex aspects or life. **This is the optimal form of attachment and has shown to be reflected in healthy, mature adult attachment as well as positive attachments while the infant grows to full maturity,**

#2- Insecure Attachment- (2 types theorized)

A. Anxious/Avoidant type- The infant fails to feel safe about their attachment to their caregiver due to a perceived lacking in the relationship-it may be due to the uncertainty or lack of stability of the caregiver's interactions with the infant. The infant will be clingy and fearful of a termination to the relationship-known in mental health as the origins of "separation anxiety".

B. Ambivalent/Avoidant type- The infant demonstrates a general lack of interest in the attachment and may even fail to respond to those instances when the caregiver enters the room. The infant, theoretically, may perceive that the caregiver has little or no interest in them thus the idea of a "safe place" does not develop. This can lead to difficulty in developing close, interpersonal relationships in adulthood as well.

#3- Disorganized Attachment- There is a perceived ongoing variance between close and no actual stable demonstration of attachment. An easy way to explain it in a general way is that the infant "doesn't know which caregiver that they are going to get on a particular day (or event). This leads to confusion over relationships-the dynamics and "rules" associated with intimacy can be blurred and high stress in adult relationships can be the outcome over this confusion.

NOTE: Considering these issues in conjunction with the following developmental models will help one understand these models:

A. THE DEVELOPMENT OF OUR MORAL CAPACITIES

Kohlberg and the Moral Developmental Model- Understanding our behavior from a moralizing basis

There are **3 general stages** of development entitled **the Pre-conventional, Conventional, and Post-Conventional Stages** of Moral Development. These 3 **general stages each have 2 parts.**

These are the two sub-sections of the Pre-Conventional State.

Part 1-We initially have our moral behaviors dictated by our fear of punishment and penalty. This is known as the **Fear & Punishment** part of our moral development.

Part 2-Then we become attached and associated with those who share our interests-act from mutual exchange. It is known as the **Good Boy/Good Girl** Stage. The goal is acceptance from parents or teachers, etc. There is no flexibility for rules and those who disobey are to be punished harshly and swiftly. Laws cannot be broken is the theme.

Stage 2 (Conventional Level) has 2 parts as well.

Stage 2/Part 1- The Mutual Interpersonal Expectations, Relationships, and Interpersonal Conformity. In this part of development people value loyalty, trust, and caring as the basis for judgments. This is the beginning of attaching the "motive" for people's actions when determining judgment and punishment.

Stage 2/Part 2- The Social Systems Morality part is primarily concerned with Social Order which is the title for this part. Laws can be changed if everyone effected are in agreement rather than having laws and inflexible and unchanging with earlier, less mature moral development. Law, social order, justice and duty are the themes in this part of the moral development mode.

Stage 3 (Post-Conventional Stage) also has 2 parts.
NOTE* - (It is not reached by many or most people with great regularity. There are frequent incidents when individuals demonstrate traits associated with them, but not consistently).

Stage 3/Part 1 is associated with **Social Contract/Individual Rights and Liberties.** This is at the core of representative government and frequently people may center on their own needs (and those who they associate with based on having shared interests), absent the universal needs of their fellow citizens in general. Otherwise, the consensus dictates policy.

Stage 3/Part 2 is the **Universal Ethical Principles** portion of the developmental model with examples given by Mother Theresa, Christ, or Martin Luther King. This is where the common good comes before the individual and is the epitome of unselfish behavior. The love for humanity is such that one is willing to sacrifice themselves for the benefit of others (even up to and including sacrificing their lives for others). This is the ultimate state of moral development and many may refuse to achieve it on a regular basis. This is because their own needs are primary in at least some of their lives-thus, not being totally committed to humanity is the result.

B. THE DEVELOPMENT OF OUR THINKING CAPACITIES

Piaget- Deductive Reasoning and Thinking as a Process

There are primarily 4 (at minimum) levels of development theorized by Jean Piaget for the rational thought/deductive reasoning processes of people and they are-

Sensorimotor- Based on manipulation of their immediate environment to get their needs met. Attempting to satisfy base existence demands.

Pre-Operational Stage- Being primarily instinctual and realizing their world through their 5 senses in order to functional minimally in infancy and early childhood. The person is seeing the world with themselves as the primary focus to consider for their world-egocentric. Getting their needs met remains the goal.

Concrete Operational Stage- (age 7 to 11). The child begins to build basic schemas to understand their world and how they are expected to function within it. They understand that different shapes can hold the same volume (conservation). They develop novel ways of understanding numbers and words (symbolism). This stages also has the feature of thoughts being made up of operations-this allows for the mind to be used rather than purely physical exertion. Thoughts are reversible. Thoughts are made up of parts, steps, or processes rather than being a singular thing, idea, etc. They can seriate things (group by size, importance, etc.)

Formal Operational thought (13 and upward) is the ability to function in a complicated manner taking into account novel situations and unusual circumstances and being able to conclude solutions that account for many different related or unrelated issues or demands. This is the mind functioning at its fullest level. (Metacognitive exercises are helpful to develop this level to a greater degree of efficiency-see Core Area 1). Unfortunately, some do not consistently operate in this manner and are unable to function in this manner (or choose to simplify things) when inappropriate to do so. Over-simplification is a core fallacy that many functional issues affecting social order and stability arise from.

C. THE DEVELOPMENTAL BLUPRINT OF OUR LIFE-SPAN DEVELOPMENT

Erik Erickson's Model of Individual Development
INTRODUCTION...

Erik Erickson devised a means of capturing our development into stages that cover the main tasks and goals for the different points in our lives. They are broad enough to cover what most people concern themselves with in their lifetimes, and, specific enough to accurately address the concerns of humanity.
No model will completely or without fail address every individual on the planet but this model appears to be accurate and a thoughtful representation of the course and progress of humans in a fairly concise manner. Some may suggest that it is outdated but still, the model, represents conservative and traditional life-span development in western culture.
Each stage is a different representation of what is "normal" as seen through the eyes of the person within the stage that they are in. Understand, the parenting style used (and their attachment pattern of the individual to their primary caregiver) are important to both their immediate and later adult development.

The First 40% of our developmental tract-

The First 40% is primarily experienced with our parents, siblings, and extended family and, later on, with our early school peers.

Erik Erickson's Model of Individual Development (Initial Stages)

Stage 1- Basic Trust vs. Mistrust (0-2 years). The infant learns that the world is a great place and people are basically good, or, that they must be careful (suspicious of other's intentions) and that people are not to be trusted. This is learned by the experiences that the infant has with the parents (and/or siblings, grandparents, etc.) and their perception of those experiences. The most significant relationship is typically the mother and the virtue that is most relative is that of Hope.

During this stage the ideals of parenting style dictate the development tract that the child works within. Equally, the attachment style that the child adopts to address their perception of their environment are important- secure, insecure, or disorganized styles of attachment have both an immediate and long-term impact on the child.

Stage 2- Autonomy vs. Shame/Doubt (2-4 years). The young child learns that they are OK or that they are bad. This is how they perceive the statements and actions of their parents (others) towards them. If you do not praise, or provide appropriate discipline, then they will be dysfunctional regarding learning about themselves. Their parents are the center of their world and the virtue that is learned is Individual Will.

During this stage it is not uncommon for the child to refer to self as a "boy" or a "girl" as they strive to identify the concept of "self" as an independent person. (They can refer to parents as "mommy" or "daddy" but cannot easily grasp them by different identities such as identifying them by their given names. Learning family relationships is an additional means of identifying self in a broader context for the child). Learning how to eat, dress self, void wastes, and the initial verbal expressions predominate. How the parent responds in the situations, (and others) will have a direct impact on development.

Stage 3- Initiative vs. Guilt (4-6 years). The child learns that they are able to take charge of circumstances and provide for themselves, or, that they are incompetent and a failure. This is the perceptual challenge that they face and the behaviors of family (most significant relationship) towards them will reinforce or determine the outcome. The virtue goal is that of Purpose (for themselves and their lives).

Making attempts to integrate into their family and providing support to the family unit such as trying to prepare a Saturday morning breakfast for their family, or, take out the trash or gather the mail are examples of efforts to participate in family life. The child needs the opportunities to participate to build their sense of family and competency. Positive experiences will help them to see initiative as a needed part of their life versus ambivalence or sense of dependence as their learned behavioral trait from this stage.

Stage 4- Industry vs. Inferiority (5-12 years). The adolescent determines that they are competent and can make it in the world as an independent, responsible citizen. If they perceive through un-reflected upon failures as a growth experience and inevitable in the process of reaching adulthood then dependency, low self-esteem, and lack of confidence is often the result. Their school peers and community are the significant relationship at this point and the goal of feeling Competent is the main virtue to be achieved.

This stage builds on the previous stages to equip the child to enter adolescence and begin as a part of a bigger family (their peers and classmates as they reach a place of independence and individual experiences for growth). Work and community service are worthy ways to assist the child to learn lessons which can help them to adjust from dependency as a child to understanding their transformation to adolescence.

Entering the 2nd 40% of our developmental tract-

The 2nd 40% is primarily experienced with both our immediate and extended family initially, as well as (later on predominately), with our peers, coworkers, and intimate relationships.

Erickson's Model (As the Individual Develops into Adulthood and Beyond)

At this point, (the age of 11) the individual theoretically goes beyond egocentric behaviors and realizes that the world is made up of more people than themselves. As they enter this stage at around 12 they come to understand that their world involves considering and acting with others best interests in mind if they are to be well-received and accepted by society.

They frequently find that they now have new found independence and increasing personal responsibilities. They now spend as much, or more, time with their friend (of the same age) and they gain their perspective from their experiences with their friends (who do not know any more about the world than they do). This is a learning process and frequently poor choices and bad decisions are a part of the growth experience. Unfortunately, this is also where, more often than not, mental health issues often find their onset due to experimentation with substances and dysfunctional personality development. Mental health disorders associated with anxiety and depressed mood find root in functioning here, as well.

The 2nd 40%- Growing and Learning to Succeed or Experiencing Failure as a Pattern-

Stage 5- Identity vs. Role Confusion (13-19 years). This is when the person explores the occupational, intimate relationship, and considers what is important (values, beliefs, and interests) to them. They make decisions of what they want to do and be. They have the initial ideas of what they expect from others (partner included) and bond with those who share their interests and ideals. The significant relationship is peers and role models and the virtue that is needed to be learned involves Fidelity and Loyalty. They spend this period going through tests regarding their friendships and relationships that will have critical, life-long impact on their world.

Sexuality and gender identity as it relates to sexuality are key aspects of development in this stage. Feelings of inadequacy or perception of self unfavorably serve to promote dysfunctional coping methods and may include experimentation with substances. Typically, in modern culture the individual is exposed to others of the same age group and they go thru life experiences absent needed parental guidance. Sometimes these experiences have detrimental effects as they may not have sufficient maturity for decision-making. Parenting style that highlights both the expectations for mature behavior while being responsive to answering touchy and sensitive questions should be hallmarks of this time frame.

Stage 6- Intimacy vs. Isolation (20-24 years). The most significant relationships are at the core of this portion of their development. The ideals associated with connectedness with their world (people who are in their lives-work, home, social, etc.) are the primary concern as well as beginning an occupational path that will lead to satisfaction of their material, social, and self-actualized goals and ambitions. This is when many marriages and intimate relationships occur with the stages leading up to this point serving to help or hinder stability. (A troubling fact is that more than 50% of marriages fail and the most often these relationships end within the first 5 years). The virtue that is most important in this stage is the experiencing appropriately of "Love".

People have, often times, found that their circle of friends to do things with shrinks due to their friends becoming involved in intimate relationship. (I have often seen that individual happiness is better realized thru intimate associations than by having possessions-isolation is identified with mental health and substance abuse typically). This is a time when joining the military, enrolling in and going away to college, relocating to another area, and the birth of children will occur for many. Those who fail to follow these, or similar tracks, may fall victim to early-adult onset of mental health issues such as anxiety or depression due to the, often, resultant isolation. These issues may cause life-long stressors unless the individual can maintain personal motivation and belief in themselves. Patience is a challenge to be overcome due to tendency to have expectations that only time and commitment to their vocation can help to be realized.

Some research indicates that females in intimate, stable relationships highly value the fulfillment of their need for safety and security in the relationship. (Having a home, available resources, and adequate financial reserves is essential to their satisfaction with the relationship). Males in intimate, stable relationships, highly prize having peace in the household. (If they can come home and find a quiet and peaceful environment then they are more satisfied with the intimate relationship).

Stage 7- Generativity vs. Stagnation (25-64 years). The significance of household (safe place to find peace from a turbulent world) and workmates (those who share a large part of your waking hours) cannot be underestimated. The success or failure is seen as a difference from climbing the mountains or being in valleys-the total time frame determines the success of failure of the person and is largely a question of their perception at a particular time in this era. The perception varies and fluctuates thus mental health issues come and go. In other instances, consistent distress based upon the person's view of their condition may occur. Those who approach a significant point along the way may feel that they are stagnate and are not measuring up to others.

They may be distressed as they view the success of others and this leads to the conclusion of their life experience as a failure with the final theorized stage known as-

Stage 8- Ego Integrity vs. Despair. (Life Perspective and Reflection of One's Life)- People usually, near what they believe to be the end period of their life, reflect on their time spent on the planet. Did I make a Difference? Did I matter? Did I accomplish anything that I am proud of, or, did I waste my life?
Having earlier considered themselves "WILL" (Is It OK to Be Me @ age (2 to 4)), they now review whether they were OK for the sum total of their lives as they consider the inevitable conclusion to their life. Then the question becomes what is, "Is there, or, what will, life after this world be like? Ultimately, positive spirituality becomes vital to allow for maximum, healthy functional stability.

They consider their impact on humanity and their families-community-and civilization. Some are not as concerned about the world as they are about their local situation whereas others are trying to make a difference for society. What you consider the way to measure your worth, as well as what was valued for your worth-this is your yardstick for how you will feel in these final years on Earth.

The Question of "What Is Normal"- Depends on the Stage and Significant Relationship at that Point-

I have found that, consistently, those who we are around early in life help us determine what is "normal" as we see the world. The behaviors of our parents and siblings, early on, are the basis for how we view our world. This goal of being "normal" fuels many behaviors and life ambitions.

When we begin attending school, we invariably have a comparison going on between ourselves and others. We share stories of our families and this begins the process of reexaminations of our "normal". Those who we associate with (moral development middle stage) and form friendships with (Erickson-Identity vs. Identity Confusion) in our adolescence are from which we identify the world.

This comparison of our family and of our peer's families leads to the new "normal". This new normal has a quality of the adolescent teaming up with other like adolescent friends ("clicks") with which to learn and experience the teenage years with This frequently, has substance use (experimentation leading to social/habit) that often serves as the basis for how we grow into adulthood to act based on what we have come to firmly believe is "normal". This is when the social "rules" (see Core Area 1- Thinking) have a great impact on the person and we become socialized through a variety of ways, e.g. marketing, tv, computer, music, sports, etc. From this backdrop, the new "normal" evolves as a set of goals, expectations, and attitudes taken into early adult life.

As we operate in our new world of work and independence (house and partner) we utilize our concept of "normal" to devise our way of operating intimately and professionally. We are impacted by our significant other as well as our colleagues and "normal" gets an additional makeover as we grow and learn more about life. This is when the substance user is typically at the addiction phase and when mental health disorders have a firm hold on the distressed individual. This is when we have the existential crisis of determining what is, and what never was, "normal". E.g. It's not about things, what appears to be fun and makes us feel good is not what we glamourized it to be earlier (addiction occurs with sometimes devastating results).

The biggest challenge for the mental health problem behaviors is whether the client is able, and willing, to let go of dysfunctional behaviors and realize that the "rules" that they have embraced from society as a young adult and teenager are really not true or even appropriate. This is the reason that, as they enter the longest stage of life (Generativity vs. Stagnation- 25-64 years), they come to realize that life is a journey and not a race. Peace, stability, and contentment matter. ("Fun" and "feeling good" do not have prime influence when maturation occurs).

Examining "Normal"- Understanding How We Operate Based on Information

The first 40% is typically about "rules for living" such as scriptural adages (Golden Rule and 10 Commandments) as well as adages about loving others, being virtuous, taking responsibility for self. These ideals frequently come from family members. This typically is the 3rd level of thinking (see Core Area 1-Thinking- re: Metacognition Exercise).

The second 40% also include marketing and media as we spend significant portions of our lives affected by these components of society. Their portrayal of society adversely affects us, often times. This is a skewed "normal" which takes time in adulthood to realize. Also, we learn from mistakes and failures in adolescence and early adulthood (typical for most) and we learn that "normal" needs further consideration.

The Confusion over "Normal"

Media marketing is attempting to sell us things and instill in us the idea that we just "have to have" something that they are presenting. Their goal is to make money for the person paying for the ad but in adolescence frequently the ads become "normal" that we base our lives on. Due to an under-developed maturity we fall victim to the portrayals that they offer, of which some are-

Beautiful is in, do you see "ugly" people on media ads? (If you you're your definition and acceptability based on physical beauty as portrayed by popular culture and the media).

Having "fun" involves substance use or sexually suggestive dress and behaviors-Is this what life is really, all about? (To get the picture watch a beer ad).

Materialism (and hedonism- feeling good) is important and we must continue to consume and buy things!
There does not seem to be much consideration for the fact that most people have limited resources that requires budgeting so that they can take care of their necessities.

Marketing isn't interested in this- "just buy and consume more" is their strategy.

COMPARISON'S OF NORMAL DURING VARIOUS STAGES OF SOCIAL LIFE (From Early Adulthood .... VERSUS .... Common, Middle Aged development)

Teenage and Early Adulthood-
Popular Media and the Effects on Culture
Music, Movies, Games, Drugs, Sex, and Materialism are the topics of Media and Marketing-either directly or indirectly (Fun and How Life Is by their Ads).
Emotional Reasoning and Outcomes (feeling good) serves as the basis of behavior. Lack of adequate self-care and precautions to ensure good health (mental and physical) due to preoccupation for fun.
This does not mean that many do not mature appropriately-this suggestion covers the expressed thinking of those who routinely present for treatment for substance and mental health concerns.

Mature Growth and Development through Experience-Middle Age and Beyond (Acceptance of personal responsibility and family obligations mandate this basis of "normal" for many).

Family is most important-frequently expressed statement I have heard reported.
Having a stable home life with adequate finances, good health, and deficit needs being met is the goal.
Planning for the future and anticipating needs and obligations.
Placing the needs of one's children and family members above self. The reasonable valuing of self vs. others.
This does not mean that most all follow this common trajectory- however, this is more consistent when substance and mental health concerns do not occur.

Most all of these traits are predicated on, or affected by, the Invincibility Fable.

THE INVINCIBILITY FABLE-

A Developmental Issue that Serves as the Cusp of Leaving Adolescent/Early Adulthood Normal and Mature Adulthood Normal.
The theoretical behavioral tendency of youth until the brain reaches full maturation around the age of 24-26 is to have an unrealistic concept of their mortality. There is a general lack of fear and less than adequate appreciation for the reality that they could die if they continue to gamble with dangerous behavior. (The orbito-frontal cortex has reached its full development potential usually by this time).

A reality from a previous core area presentation (Behaviors- Core Area 3) suggests that the behavioral cycle includes a point known as social/habit regarding substance use and mental health disordered onset. The typical point where this occurs is often associated with the period of time prior to the full maturation of the brain whereby the person is aware of the full danger to their personage from social/habit state of substance use.

By the time that they person reaches the place to fully appreciate the dangers of substance use they are entering addiction where they have real problems controlling their use. This is also when mental health distress seems to reach the initial treatment stage as the person realizes their need for the treatment.

The Challenge to Achieve "Normal" Viewing the Lifespan Development Model-

If parents and siblings during the initial stages of development have given you bad examples then your sense of "normal" is skewed even in its initial stages.

If you over-depend on your peers in your school years then you may develop a potentially dangerous sense of "normal" (generally fun oriented lacking mature judgment).

Add to it the media and marketing who are trying to realize a profit rather than you immature idea that ads are based on "truth", then "normal" is skewed as you enter adulthood.

Your beginning years of independence and being armed with all of these above scenarios then "normal" is distorted at worst, and problematic at best. You have to address multiple issues associated with adult life that may not have been adequately addressed from parents, extended family, or other role models.

You may then arrive at the end of the invincible fable time frame with addiction and mental health issues firmly established. Then you realize that you must try to achieve good mental health. This is the challenge for mental health treatment and your attempts to be "normal".

(6-A)

CORE AREA SIX- Questions for Discussion and Self-Assessment

1. Name 3 important things that happened in your childhood years that you believe had a negative impact on your adulthood.

2. Name 3 important things that happened in your childhood years that you believe had a positive impact on your adulthood.

3. When did you first have a sexual experience- what age and do you have a positive memory of that experience?

4. Do you think that it is important to have both parents in the home during your school years- Why, or, Why Not?

5. In your teenage years, what was the substance use practices in your household?

6. Did your family members have mental health issues and do you feel that they have been inherited? Or, are these issues learned behaviors?

7. What is the birth order in your family (your brothers and sisters-what order) and where are you in that order? Does it have an effect on how your grew up?

8. What is your definition or description of "normal" as it relates to an appropriate lifestyle, and why?

CORE AREA SEVEN
The Perspective of Addiction (and Mental Health Recovery)-
THE ADDICT AND THE RECOVERY PROCESS

An Introduction and Premise

I have been working in various capacities with addicts for practically 20 years and have come to recognize that, in general, the addict has a mindset and perspective that misrepresents common concepts associated with living.

These misrepresentations have occurred, in many instances, out of the necessity that requires this practice in order to avoid having the addict face the reality of their addictive personality patterns. They often hide their use through deception. These misrepresentations are fundamentally dysfunctional and represent a way of approaching their daily lifestyle so that they can continue in their way of living and ignore the painful reality of their circumstances. This is demonstrated in the practice of using to hide self from the results of their addiction. (?)

The Vicious Cycle-A Never-Ending Loop

The basis for use can be traced to several routes to arrive at addiction. The routes are numerous and vary widely depending on the addict you talk to. However, there are some that are most common and include-

Self-medicating behaviors to mask anxiety, depression, or health problems with the pain/distress associated with each being numbed.

Wanting to "feel good" or to "feel better". This is typically unrealistic in light of their circumstances with only a distraction from a problem(s) that are only worse due to inattention to dealing with life on life's terms.

The problem with either of these scenarios (or others such as grief, loneliness, financial insolvency, relationship issues) is that their existence continues unchanged (usually) as a result of the self-medicating practice that attempts to hide them.

Further, the continued use makes these issues worse and also allows for additional problems relating to addiction such as loss of job, partners, children, criminal prosecution, or health (mental and physical) problems. Ultimately, this increased stress may include death or imprisonment due committing crimes under the influence or to gain the resources to purchase more drugs. Of course, this doesn't include loss of family, home, or livelihood.

Drug Abuse effects multiple issues-a few include pregnancy and domestic violence. Please consider these issues with this brief address:

THE EFFECTS OF DRUGS ON THE DEVELOPMENT OF THE INFANT DURING PREGNANCY (and after birth).

Cigarette Smoking- Prenatal exposure to cigarette smoke has been linked to derogatory effects on arousal, attention (RAS), as well as cognitive deficits in humans. (The effects are on the Reticular Activation System (RAS) which impacts both the prenatal infant and the adult). For the unborn increased levels of arousal occur from the nicotine receptors that may cause negative attentional dysregulation later in life.

Substance Abuse (in general)- Increases the risk of miscarriage, can cause migraines, seizures, and high blood pressure (all of which affect the natal development of the unborn baby).

There is a 2 to 3 (X's) greater risk of stillborn birth due to smoking cigarettes and/or marijuana, taking prescription pain medications, and illegal drugs during pregnancy.

Withdrawal- may occur for the newborn due to the mother's use of opioids, alcohol, caffeine, and some prescription sedatives. The type and severity of withdrawal varies.

Finally, research indicates that substance use and abuse for the pregnant mother can incur long-term or fatal effects for the infant which include:

- Low birth weight
- Birth defects
- Small head size
- Premature birth
- Sudden Infant Death Syndrome (SIDs)
- Developmental delays
- Problems with learning, memory, and emotional control.

NOTE: Drugs can also be in breast milk so, the threat of damage does not end with birth of the baby. In addition, the continued drug use after birth means, often, that the need for the substance negatively affects the availability of adequate resources or time spent in appropriate parenting. My experience is that the addict is committed to drug acquisition, rather than having a primary directed attention to the infant.

Addiction is not only the act of using substances of abuse- it is a lifestyle. It must be changed to where other's interests, as well as concerns for stable living, take precedent over continued use and abuse for personal emotional satisfaction.

***Some sobering statistics to know concerning alcohol and drug abuse and domestic violence. Changing your lifestyle not only increases prosocial behaviors for the addict-it may result in less likelihood for abuse in the household.*

Here are a few facts concerning Substance Abuse and Domestic Violence

- Regular alcohol abuse is a leading risk factor for partner violence.
- Battering incidents are more severe with greater injuries when alcohol abuse is involved.
- Alcoholic women are more likely to report that they had physical & emotional abuse than nonalcoholic women.
- Abused women are 15 times more likely to abuse alcohol and 9 more times likely to abuse drugs.
- 69% of women in treatment for substance abuse reported sexual abuse as children or adolescence.
- 61% of domestic violence offenders also have a substance abuse problem. ……………………………………….. (information provided by SAMHSA, 2017).

THE ADDICTION RECOVERY PROCESS-
A progression of experiences to address -Introduction to the Topic;

My experience in the field of substance abuse has led me to believe that there are various stages, steps, or hurdles that are consistent to be overcome. These steps constitute a "process" and, by addressing these steps, the addict may be better prepared to navigate through these hurdles to abstinence. What follows are things that the addict must be prepared for-awareness equips one to guard themselves. This process follows:

The Addict's Recovery- "It's A Process"

Denial…………………………………………………………………………………
The initial and most difficult task for the addict to address when they even begin to consider treatment and abstinence is to admit that they have a problem. They choose to deny their substance abuse unless, often times, they hit rock bottom. Much literature points to the fact that often time the addict must go to their absolute lowest before they take the necessary steps to get clean and sober.
A true support for this idea is to ask an addict that attended their first few AA/NA meetings and give you a description of how they felt about identifying themselves as an "addict" when they shared. This is a hard pill to swallow for the prideful person who must face themselves.

Blaming...

Most addicts will explain their newly admitted abusing tendencies by identifying someone else as the reason for their use.

It is usually always someone's fault other than themselves. Getting them to admit to their associates (and especially to themselves) that they alone are responsible for their addiction is a time-consuming process that requires much work on the part of the entire group (in treatment) to convince them that it is indeed OK to be at fault.

They usually are so sensitive to criticism that they see the obligation to acknowledge their self as the cause very difficult.

Embarrassment...

After the addict accepts that they have a problem and that it is their fault, they consistently are embarrassed. It is hard to face the humility needed on their part to approach treatment from the position of being in need of help.

A common behavior for the addict is that they have "got this" in general as an approach to life. To acknowledge that they are in need of others to overcome their self-responsible behaviors is a threat to their independence and self-esteem. To them, their positive feelings about self may be all that they have and the thought of giving them up is unbearable-this may be the most embarrassing part of the process.

The additional concern with embarrassment is that they may, instead, feel shame. This is part of an existential controversy that goes something like this-

Embarrassment usually results in the person trying to make amends and improve/repair the damage, on the other hand, shame is usually demonstrated by hiding and avoiding letting anyone know of their behaviors.

In the instance of shame, an additional step is needed to convince the addict that there is no reason to feel shame unless other activities that harmed others intentionally were at stake. Even then, realizing that we are all human and will make mistakes as a definition of being human should be considered by both the addict and those who help.

THE RECOVERY PROCESS- (Note: At any of these steps the addict may return to their addiction due to their perceived inability to continue in treatment. They, then often surrender to (and return to) their addiction).

IN EARLY TREATMENT

The addict has a few weapons still left at their disposal when they enter treatment that they use when they demonstrate that they are not totally invested in treatment. They may often feel forced to be there but they can still passive-aggressively resist change. They will hold back and resist total commitment to rehabilitation. They usually rely on-

(1) Hostility to Criticism
(2) Resentments
(3) Avoiding Personal Responsibility

Hostility to Criticism...

A common ploy is to minimize, maximize, justify, excuse, or deflect (behavioral techniques- Core Area 3) any deep probing of their use and abusing practices and history. The most likely statement is to focus outward on others in the group who have "done much worse" or "were selfish and let someone (named) down". By doing this the attention is away from them-not realizing that by doing this they are denying themselves the opportunity to grow and gain strength in their own recovery. It is not uncommon for this individual to go to the point of blows or verbal abuse (or passive-aggression) to take the heat off of themselves.

Resentments...

These represent the potential triggers for relapse as the addict thinks that others "had it in for me" or "were jealous of me" or "treated me like...", etc.
Usually they see "tough love" as a personal slight by those who they thought they could "depend on" and not knowing that it pained those people who had to practice "tough love". The problem is that the addict is focusing on what they wanted rather than the fact that this was maybe the only option left to get them to come to their senses. Relationships, job loss, or lack of understanding by others that has led to some pitfall for the addict is misinterpreted as having a malicious intent.

Avoiding Personal Responsibility...

This is perhaps the most difficult pill for the addict to swallow because they often hold jobs, pay bills, and shuffle multiple responsibilities while misappropriating their money and time to fuel their addiction.
Two questions come to mind to address the addict's defensive posture-

(1) "If you could do all of those things and still abuse substances what would you have been able to do if you weren't using?", and,
(2) Part of having personal responsibility is to take proper care of your own health (mental and physical). Since the pendulum swings forward and backwards (only briefly remain stationary). "Are you improving or regressing with your substance abuse?"

THE INEVITABLE HURDLES THAT THE NEW TREATMENT ADDICT MUST OVERCOME

While the addict is in the early part of treatment and the previously mentioned traits are being demonstrated, the addict who is taking in the material and examining their own life will have various distortions of language as they relate to them personally. These terms identify where they are in spite of their outward use of defensive postures. They include-

(1) Unforgiving of Self
(2) Low Self-Esteem
(3) Defeated Personality ("I will never get through this").
(4) Negative Self-Concept ("I am an addict").
(5) Hopelessness ("Why not use, it does not matter anyway" or "who cares anyway?")

Unforgiving of self..
Typically, numerous people who are close to the addict (or were close) have been hurt. The addict feels guilty for having been detrimental and having hurt others. They do not see how they can ever make it up or renew their previous relationships. They conclude that they should give up and resume abusing substances.

The point that they must come to discover is that "you can never step into the same river twice" so that they will realize that their relationship does not have to be the same-different may actually be better or improved.

Low Self-Esteem..
While the full effect of their addiction is becoming known to them by their own reflection they do not see themselves as having any value. This is dangerous. Self-harm can occur when the person sees the full effect (usually exaggerated by their own embarrassment and shame) of their addiction.

The true test of being engaged in treatment fully is to actively take steps to improve your overall life while learning about yourself so that you can experience success while growing in therapy. The small steps of achieving success will serve to lead you forward and avoid relapse due to not wanting to mess up your recovery. Also-avoid concentrating on the invariable failures that will also occur.

Defeated personality..
Recovery is not a smooth, continual process forward and upward. There are continual tests and bumps in the road. When the problems occur (and they will) the typical attitude is to have the irrational though process of saying "I knew this was going to happen, it never fails", or, "this always happens to me-so what is the use". The fact is that this is irrational thinking-nothing more.

This is something that takes a sponsor and cups of coffee in the middle of the night when you would rather relapse and say "screw it, why bother anyway".

Negative Self-Concept..
There is a general distasteful perception of addicts as those who sleep in the park or under a bridge. They appearance is generally considered poor and they usually are devious in many ways or so it is thought by society in their portrayals

on TV and in movies. When an addict faces their past and looks at themselves they fall into the trap of giving themselves this self-concept. This is damaging and potentially fatal to their recovery.

Truth is that addicts are just human beings who have used inappropriate coping skills to deal with life-they are human and are lovable and precious children of the same God who loves all of his creation. They need to be at peace with themselves-no one is perfect.

Hopelessness..

This situation is only partially revealed at this point and, although more manageable, it grows as the person becomes self-aware. The addict loses the barrier to personal reflection that their addiction and, later, defensive tools had provided. They initially, see that their withdrawal symptoms and "feelings" as troublesome. Later, as they realize the fuller effects of their dual-diagnosis issues of anxiety, depression, etc. their hopelessness further expands.

THE UNMASKED MENTAL HEALTH PROBLEMS PREVIOUSLY SELF-MEDICATED ARE NOW IN THE OPEN-

Here are some of the ongoing battles that are part of the misconception of symbolic concepts for words that are a problem for the addict to deal with while they also face their demons trying to sabotage their recovery. Remember, often they have been self-medicating to address these demons-now they don't have the substances to numb the pain.

(1) Anxiety and anxious behaviors.
(2) Depression (sometimes with grief, loss of partner, job, or health related pain).

Anxiety has the chief components of worry, restlessness, and an inability to relax self (mind or body). This translates to stress and lack of sleep. When one stops using substances there is a period of time when their sleep issues get worse or are no longer masked so that the full effect of sleeplessness is realized. This is when meditating and breathing exercises are vital.

Further, the substance use/abuse has kept the cycle of anxiety going, it will take some time before the lack of use will take effect and mitigate the symptoms associated with anxiety. Be patient and know you are in a real fight. See a medicating prescriber for their opinion as to whether you may need short-term help-be proactive, seek out professional assistance instead of acting alone.

People who are depressed frequently resort to substance to help them "ignore" their depressed state. What puzzles me is that of the substance use has a negative effect on dopamine and serotonin neurotransmitter production and firing. This ensures that they will remain depressed. So, what were they thinking?

Along with full experiencing of the diagnostic symptoms of depression and anxiety comes further experienced problems-

(1) Hopelessness (continued, to an even greater degree than before)
(2) Anger and Irritability/Negativity

Hopelessness..
At this stage of treatment hopelessness takes on the additional quality of being associated with relapse, self-harm, and permanent disability and death. The use of the 12 Step and AA/NA theme of spirituality as a central portion of the model was not by chance. Having faith and a knowledge that there is a God of your understanding gives coping skills because there is someone who had your back and you have something to hold on to for your future. This reality makes it easier to realize that there is a future and quitting is not optional. It may be this straw, pending an extended recovery with added strength, which will see the addict through to a better place.

Anger & Irritability/Negativity..
I have seen sorrow and anger as off-shoots of each other with the person going from crying to fits of anger. Things get broken, people assaulted, and a resignation that the behavior was wrong with relapse as the outcome, after all- "what's the use".
The fact that your body has to adjust to the absence of the substances leave you irritable is obvious. The negativity is the part of this which the addict is the last to realize when they are in a relationship with others who are trying to support them. The constant doubt and over-sensitivity to failure and mistakes haunts the recovering addict and he/she must realize that "Rome was not built in a day".

THE FRUITS OF RECOVERY- WHEN THE END OF THE TUNNEL BECOMES IN FOCUS

When the addict gets to the point in treatment where they begin to realize some significant, obvious changes in themselves- they begin to grow. Some addiction theory states that, at the time that the drug use began (frequently as a teenager), their maturity process stopped. (They are still a teenager maturity wise it is theorized). Remember, statistically approximately 7 out of 10 addicts have significant personality disordered behavioral traits at minimum (or actual diagnosed personality disorders).

My approach to treatment finds it important for the addict to have experienced some early treatment successes such as securing a job, apartment, car, etc. They have lived, often times, with lacking due to their drug abuse and now experience success that encourages them to continue to work on their recovery. Some of the things that occur at this point (and are real blessings to see as a therapist) include-

(1) Gratitude
(2) Acceptance
(3) Honesty
(4) The end of Selfishness & the beginning of Selflessness

Gratitude……………………………………………………………………………..
One of the first things that the client shares with you in private is how grateful that they are to have whatever they are fortunate to have salvaged from their past or of whom they still are in positive interpersonal relationships with. They come to understand that it is not always about having more but, rather, about being satisfied and content with what they already have been blessed to possess. The come to appreciate their "chance" to have a better life and look forward positively, yet cautiously, to better days ahead.

Acceptance……………………………………………………………………………
Not only does the addict accept himself in spite of his past and look forward to the future with promise and hope, they accept their faults, mistakes, and errors and realize that they are still growing.
Acceptance requires the person to see themselves realistically and free of any irrational, defensive, or excusing/blaming behaviors that they have relied upon in the past. They learn that it is not necessary to make excuses and they rely, instead, upon-

Honesty……………………………………………………………………………..
From the beginning of their substance use (usually as a teenager) and moving forward they have felt it necessary to lie about their use and themselves in most situations.
For what may be the first time in their life for quite some time they are able to be honest and not have to feel that they have something to hide.
It is a freeing and refreshing thing to them and they will find so much contentment in just being open and honest without hiding themselves and what they think, feel, and experience. Honesty has indeed set them free.

Selflessness……………………………………………………………………………..
The real breakthrough occurs when the addict in recovery realizes that they have changed and have finally made it to the point of saying "put me in coach, I am ready to play". This is when others now matter more than themselves. Their wives, significant others, children, family members, and friends (who are truly friends rather than drug buddies) have had to take a back seat to the recovering addict for a long time. Now, the recovering addict realizes the inequity of their past relationships. The addict takes matter into their own hands in order to treat those who have had faith in them with the kindness and love that the supporters knew the recovering addict had inside of them. Now the addict is no longer afraid to

open up and face those who had supported the addict. They now face life on life's terms.

CORE AREA SEVEN- Self Reflection & Recovery Issues Considerations

Spend some time reflecting on the terms and concepts associated with the Core Area recovery stages- the issues to be navigated through, and provide your insight regarding personal experiences and reflections. What comes to mind when you consider;

1. Denial of having a problem behavior or addiction?
2. Who did you blame for the problem or addiction?
3. Have you been told that you lack personal responsibility- in what ways?
4. Do you feel hopeless due to problem behaviors or addiction? Or, have have you ever felt that way-when and why?
5. Do you feel that criticism can be constructive-when is it constructive and when is it not so? (Are you just being overly sensitive?)
6. Do you have resentments against others because of their treatment of you- and, why? What was their explanation for their actions that you resent? (Can you see that the explanation may be legitimate?)
7. Did you try substances to self-medicate, to feel good, or not feel bad? (If there is a different reason- what was the reason?)
8. Do you think that feeling good requires drugs or problem behaviors?
9. Is gratitude and acceptance necessary for positive recovery experiences and continued abstinence?
10. Discuss selflessness. Explain what the concept means to you and how do you demonstrate it to others?
11. Are you able to be honest with those who are aware of your addition or problem behaviors? If not, why?

CORE AREA EIGHT
THE BRAIN-
Site of Drug Use and Mental Health Dysfunction's Origin
CONCEPTUALIZATIONS-SEEING THE BRAIN IN OUR MINDS:

The Learning Objectives for this Core Area:

This material should equip the reader with the general knowledge of how substances effect the functioning of the brain. A basic explanation of how we operate and of the potential long-term effects of substance abuse is addressed in concluding this section.
Substance use does not provide a "feel good", rather, a dysfunction to the brain's operation-this is the reality which is under represented in culture.

A Visual Picture: The brain can be categorized as consisting of 3 sections (from front to back) or in 2 sections (from left to right as one sees a person's frontal face view).
If you look at the person from the front face view (from right to left) it consists of the right hemisphere and the left hemisphere (the brain as it is conceptualized as consisting of 2 parts).
If you look at the brain from the front of the person (their face and backwards to the back of the head) then it consists of 3 parts (Frontal Lobe, Mid-Brain, and the Hind-Brain).
Additionally, you may consider the brain based upon its outside area-gray matter (Cerebral Cortex) and the inside/interior region (white matter). Just as a point of interest, the brain is theorized to be approximately 70% made up of fatty based tissue.

A Hemispheric Look at the Brain and its Operations (LEFT TO RIGHT)

Left Hemisphere (left side of the face going towards the back):

This side is responsible for these operations-
Sequential Analytical brain functioning-the systematic and logical interpretation of information. Interpretation and production of symbolic information (language, math, abstract and absolute reasoning). In this hemisphere, memory is stored in a language format.

Right Hemisphere- (right side of the face going towards the back):

This side is responsible for these operations-
Holistic Functioning:
The processing of multi-sensory input simultaneously to provide a "holistic" picture of one's environment. Visual spatial skills, holistic functions such as dance, gymnastics, are coordinated by the right hemisphere. Memory is stored in auditory, visual, and spatial modalities in the right hemisphere.

A More Complicated Categorization of the Brain

The brain, as seen from the 3 parts (front to back) as well as from the 2 half division (side to side-right to left), is a more accurate means of understanding the general brain structure.
The left and right hemisphere division (front portion) of the 3 part breakdown is known as the Frontal Lobe (Right Frontal Lobe and Left Frontal Lobe).

The Frontal Lobe division is described as being the portion of the brain which accomplishes "executive functioning" for the person. As such, this portion is what serves to make decisions and effect actions based on those decisions-then, activating various other areas of the brain to accomplish these decisions.

THE RIGHT AND LEFT FRONTAL LOBES- What They Do (The Brain's Executive Functioning Roles)

Thinking and Memory (cataloging and filing functions as well as some memory storage).

Movement is orchestrated by the executory operation of the frontal lobe. (By gender-girls usually have superior fine motor skills. early on, while boys, early on, have superior gross motor skills. **Storage area for motor patterns and for voluntary activities. Language and motor speech is managed in this region also.**

The Rail Switch Function- Understanding Split-Brain Malfunction and the Corpus Callosum-

A simple yet effective way to visualize the brain is to look at a shelled, yet undamaged, walnut. The walnut visually represents the basic view one gets at looking at the outer brain. Inside the shell is a dark, shell "skin" between the half areas of the walnut. This is-in an easy manner-how we can visualize the portion of the brain that is called the Corpus Callosum.

The Corpus Callosum has the function of sending and directing signals from one hemisphere of the brain to the other hemisphere so that they can work together to get things accomplished that the brain determines what needs to be done.

When the Corpus Callosum is damaged the brain does not have the ability to work in tandem so, the person has, in effect, a split-brain disorder (the inability causes many problems; especially with verbal knowledge/expression-e.g. Wernicke (rt. Side) and Broca (lf. Side) areas of the frontal lobe area.

THE MID-BRAIN REGION (From the outside working inward as an additional way of understanding the Brain)-

The outer shell area of the mid-brain, from right to left across the brain, consists of multiple "lobes" (regions) that have different, important functions for the individual. This outer portion is also known as the Cerebral Cortex. Some major lobes include, (1 on each "side"/hemisphere; X2 total):

Lower side (Parietal Lobe) accomplishes the sensory input to the brain-discriminates between the sense based information while allowing us to have a proper orientation to our own bodies. Damage to this area leaves us unable to recognize our bodies, be disoriented to our environment, and unable to write.

Middle side/back (Occipital Lobe) accomplishes visual sense input discriminations for the brain-allow one to interpret what they see. Damage to either side causes loss of vision in the opposite eye (temporary damage such as "flash of light" or "stars").

Top of mid-brain region (Temporal Lobe) multiple functions in this lobe such as auditory, expressed behavior, and receptive language speech interpretation. The process of retrieval of memory is managed by the temporal lobe. This is generally referred to as the accumulative location for procedural and declarative memory.

These described lobes are the outer shell of the mid-brain. Inside them within the exterior region of the brain are other components that allow us to have emotional context to our world.

The Mid-Brain Region-The Inner Region-
Due the opening of the mouth and the downward curve of the skull the middle of the brain is narrowed with the middle serving as the connector junction of the brain to the spine. This is accomplished at the junction of the back edge of the mid-brain and the frontal area of the hind-brain. (Similar to a kidney shape if you will). This narrowed area midbrain is location includes the **Limbic System**.
The human traits of rage and fear, sexual drive, and emotional behaviors come from this region. A primary component of this inner, midbrain region is the **Papez Circuit**. This circuit **is made up of the Hippocampi, Amygdala, and Hypothalamus.**

Mid-Brain- (The Papez Circuit "Our Emotional Center")

The Hippocampi has the responsibility of the emotional reasoning and supplies the signal that activates the Hypothalamus to give the physiological meaning to our conceptual emotional reasoning (fear, joy, pain, happiness). As such, the Hypothalamus is the memory center for our emotional experiences. The actual expression of these, and other emotions, is accomplished by the Amygdala. The Amygdala is the largest and most prominent element of the Papez Circuit and accounts for the expression, in actual experience, of being "overcome with emotion". In the psychological conceptual basis, this is called the Yerkes-Dobson Principle.

Further examination of the Hypothalamus

The hypothalamus can be understood as the anterior (outer) or posterior (inner) portion dissecting-
The anterior hypothalamus has the responsibility for parasympathetic activities such as temperature and metabolism.
The posterior hypothalamus is responsible for our "fight or flight" behavior. This concept is our cataloging of a situation and whether we should run or stand our ground. This serves as the feeding center and the central location for the addiction issue of the "dopamine reward center". We enjoy the release of the dopamine neurotransmitter in our Papez Circuit and thus, we consume substances of abuse to release this dopamine in this center. This is the crux of the theory of addiction as a disease concept.

RAS-Reticular Activating System (A seldom discussed portion of the Mid-Brain)

The RAS is responsible for the sleep-wake, circadian rhythm cycle of the individual. This cycle monitors and manages the sleep and rest needs and must be maintained in a consistent manner to avoid stress on the cognitive structures to avoid MH issues. Specifically, the RAS monitors arousal from sleep, wakefulness, and attention. This is the portion of the brain that is activated by our morning ritual of drinking caffeine products.

THE HIND BRAIN- (Our Prehistoric Past as a Part of our Life Continuing Ability)

The back portion of the brain (located as the back 1/3 of the skull) is the Hind-Brain. It has the function of involuntary, life-essential functions for the body such as blood pressure, breathing, heart rate, blood vessel dilation and contractions, and reflexes such as coughing, sneezing, swallowing, and vomiting. **The Cerebellum, Pons, and Medulla make up the major parts of the Hindbrain.**

The **Cerebellum** has the responsibility of assisting in shifting one's attention from visual to auditory stimuli. It assists in the full awareness of pleasure/pain responses, and coordinates sensory information along with motor control so that things are precisely, timely, and coordinated accomplished movements. (When you are clumsy this is not happening).

The **Pons** is the chief manager of receiving and coordinating information from the brainstem (Pons) that arrives from the spinal column that then passes to the brain proper. **Connecting the Pons (upper brainstem) to the spinal column is the Medulla (lower brainstem-also known as the Medulla Oblongata.** These two portions that make up the total brainstem are vital as they are the originating point for sets of cranial nerves that leave the brain to the body (bypassing the spinal column). Cranial nerves 5-8 (Pons) and 9-12 (Medulla) take care of all of the vital body functions already discussed as well as facial sensations, biting-chewing-swallowing, eye rotation, facial expressions, transmission of sound from ears to brain, breathing intensity-frequency, and equilibrium, and posture.

The Elixir that makes the parts work-Neurotransmitters

The brain is made up of billions of brain cells and, like all cells, they have a center with the matter which make the cell viable. In the brain cells these center chemicals are known as neurotransmitters. They work by "firing" a signal between the cells to accomplish the function of the part of the brain where the firing takes place.

The cells look like they have tiny "hairs" from the cell center and these "hairs" are hollow (dendrites). The neurotransmitter travels down the dendrite canals and fires at the synaptic cleft (the ending of the dendrite). This signal process takes a split second and the activity, movement, stimuli interpretation, etc. is complete.

When the neurotransmitters are not present, not in sufficient quantities, or over-abundant due to substance abuse (or organic dysfunction) then the firing does not properly take place. This is the advent of MH and SA related disorders. This is also a proximal cause for some diseases such as dementia, Parkinson's, Huntington's, etc.

The Effects of Substances on the Neurotransmitters-4 Basic Effects

When the neurotransmitter is operating properly it is at a balanced position. When it is not balanced, it operates in one of 4 ways-either because of defect or because of substance effect. As stated earlier in this manual, neurotransmitters either are antagonistic, partial-antagonist, agonist, or partial-agonist. In short, the neurotransmitter is either ceasing, greatly slowed, greatly elevated, or off the charts. This is the essential effect of drugs on the person when they, otherwise, are operating at a base, normal rate. When they are not and are not using substances-providers prescribe psychopharmacology regimens to alter the balance to achieve the base, normal rate. This is a theoretical basis for prescribing medications to assist clients in dealing with MH issues such as depression, anxiety, etc.

The Neurotransmitters-An overview

The neurotransmitters follow basic functional operations such as working as an exciting or sedating action, or, capable of accomplishing both based on the way and extent the neurotransmitter operates at.
Different neurotransmitters are used by different brain cell operations that are located within specific brain areas or lobes. Each has a different purpose and supports the operation of the person by having the brain operate with these neurotransmitters sending the appropriate signals throughout the body to make the brain's signaled behaviors occur.

The Neurotransmitters-An overview

Briefly stated, the specific neurotransmitter and the responsibility of that neurotransmitter is:

Acetylcholine-motor control, learning, memory, sleep, dreams.
Epinephrine-energy.
Norepinephrine-arousal, vigilance.
Serotonin-emotion, impulses, dream.
Dopamine-reward, motivation, motor control.
Gaba (abbreviated)-inhibit action potential.
Glutamate-enhance action potential, learning, memory.
Endorphins-reward, pain reduction.
Substance p-pain perception, mood.

Note-there are potentially over a 100 neurotransmitters- the above are most prominent.

When the neurotransmitters are affected by biological defect or from substance abuse, the following happens (dysfunctional neurotransmitter activity and the problem result):

Acetylcholine- Alzheimer's symptoms, deterioration of memory, reasoning and language skills. Muscle spasms and trembling. (It is estimated that almost 90% of the brain's acetylcholine is absent in those with Alzheimer's disorder).
Dopamine- Parkinson's disease. Difficulty starting and stopping voluntary movements. Tremors at rest, stooped posture, rigidity, and poor balance.

Schizophrenia. Disruptions in cognition and emotion, delusions, hallucinations, disorganized speech, and inappropriate social skills.

Epinephrine (adrenaline) - sleep disturbances, temperature regulation, hormonal imbalances, racing heart, and blood pressure or other involuntary body functioning.

Gaba- Chronic insomnia, racing mind, anxiety disorders.

Norepinephrine- Mood disorders, depression, fatigue, and anxiety.

Endorphins- Severe mood swings, flat affect, pain disorder.

Serotonin- Mood disorders, depression, impulsive behavior, aggressiveness, suicide.

The Neurotransmitters-What is Not Working Properly from SA/MH dysfunction?

Thus far the brain has been discussed as well as the neurotransmitters that operate to fulfill the messenger functions to activate our existence. What parts are not working when what neurotransmitters are negative affected is the missing topic follow-up. Here are the general answers-

Midbrain (emotions, reward, movements, attention, memory sleep, sexual desire, appetite, sensory processing, mood, anxiety) affected by dopamine, serotonin, norepinephrine (over or under abundance). The drugs that are the culprit include cocaine, meth, amphetamines, LSD, and/or Ecstasy.

Spinal cord and throughout the brain (affects practically all areas in different amounts or degrees-neuron activity, anxiety, memory, and anesthesia). Endogenous opioids (endorphin and encephalin neurotransmitters), Glutamate, and Gaba neurotransmitters are affected by-
Heroin, morphine, prescription pain-killers ((Oxycodone), Ketamine, Phencyclidine, Alcohol, sedatives, and tranquilizers). These drugs affect the above mentioned neurotransmitter operations in varying extents.

Hippocampus, cerebral cortex, thalamus, basal ganglia, cerebellum are all affected by nicotine and marijuana.

NOTE: These areas listed in this and the preceding pages are associated with the dopamine reward center indirectly or directly, thus, the use of drugs in general have a result that includes the dopamine reward center/system as the <u>motivation</u> AND <u>benefactor</u> of the substance abuse. In short, the <u>cycle is circular</u> and is mutually supported and increased to form "addiction" and is evidenced by "cravings" and "urges" as part of the language used to describe this <u>cyclical pattern of use which is reinforcement, intensification, use, reinforcement, intensification, etc.</u>

Changes to the Brain from Chronic Drug Use- the "Price of Addiction"

Initially, drug use has the intoxicants wear off and leave the brain with a cessation of use. However, chronic drug use destroys cellular structures and functioning with long-lasting or permanent effects.

Cell structures can replicate the effects of drug use thus the drug use does not allow for the same or equally intensive effects that it previously did. This leads to increased amounts and number of times for that use to compensate for this lack of experiencing the "first buzz". Addicts have never reported revisiting their initial high has been my experience by their self-report.

The drug use may increase and alter the dendrite production that normally is reserved for new learning by the individual. Thus leading to increased "learning of drug dependence" from expanded drug-related dendrite production which, in turn, **leads to further addiction.**

Some drug use has toxicity to the serotonin neurotransmitter (depressed state may result) causing disruption that underlies long-lasting memory problems (meth, ecstasy). The drug use may also damage to dopamine neurotransmitter sending cells to cause defects in thinking and motor skills (amphetamines).

Abstinence may allow for regeneration and some recovery but there is no clear research to show that full recovery does occur.

SUMMARY and CONCLUSION-

The purpose of the Dual Diagnosis program (mental health and substance use co-occurring disorders) is to highlight material that may be helpful to the group participant for a change from their substance abuse to abstinence. Further, by understanding the tools and techniques to address the mental health issues underlying the substance use, the goal is recovery.

The most important and essential question that is to be asked for any of the sessions is- Was It [substance abuse] Worth It? Realizing the obvious answer is the beginning to the process of recovery.

Since it is not possible to identify what material will be most advantageous to each client in treatment, I have applied the "kitchen sink" approach. I have included a full coverage on a range of information that will hopefully find application to the broadest audience. I hope that this material is able to lead the client to examine, understand, and make the appropriate changes to eventually lead to abstinence from substances or recovery from mental health dysfunction. In order to do so, one must avoid "intellectualizing the materials" and, rather, "conceptualize the materials for their daily life". In short, apply what you have read and considered it for your own life and individual circumstances.

The idea behind my presentation is not to hammer away that one is an addict, rather, here is how you can understand, know, and consider how you got here. Further, how you can correct yourself by first having personal awareness. Then, realizing what caused your situation so that you can walk back the process to correct as appropriate. I hope for every client's positive outcome.

A point made within the sessions was that our symbolism (language, etc.) and the interpretation of it makes all the difference. We attach "fun" and "feeling good" to the substance use rather than a clear, intelligent understanding of the substances based on what they actually do to us. Reality is that we are only manipulating our brains and over, or under, stimulating ourselves away from how we were intended to function. Understand, using drugs is a distraction away from considering ourselves and thinking about our thinking as a metacognition skill. The real question is "What were you thinking?"

WORKSHEETS- Aides to the Manual for Development of Skills

The worksheets are added to this manual to reinforce the various skills and help the reader to practice the suggested functional skills for more effective daily living (improved quality of life).

Practice them often and work towards making their use "automatic" in your daily life. Once they have become second nature you will find that they assist you to be more effective in your thinking-thus in your actions you will improve your chances of success.

With added success comes an improved self-concept and elevated self-esteem. Additionally, using effective problem-solving and methodical approaches to your thinking can enhance your cognitive capacities. Point being, you will be experiencing self-improvement which is the reason for these exercises and the goal of treatment. You will develop a more analytical approach to your thinking.

The goal is "Good Mental Health".

(WK-1)

META-COGNITION ("Thinking about Your Thinking")

Level Of Thinking	Reasoning
1st Level- What Blurted Out Thought Did you Say?	Why You Said It-
2nd Level-What experience, lesson, etc. made you Say That Blurt Out the Thought?	Question- What is The Accuracy of the Thought?
3rd Level- What Were You Taught as You Grew Up About This?	Does the 1st and 2nd Level Find Support from the 3rd Foundational Level of Thinking?
EITHER THE 1ST AND 2ND ARE SUPPORTED BY THE 3RD – OR NOT. Yes OR No?	DO YOU CHANGE YOUR THINKING OR GO WITH WHAT YOU WERE TAUGHT? THINK!!!!

(WK- 2)

DIAPHGRAMATIC BREATHING- A Checklist Approach

THIS METHOD IS ABSOLUTELY ESSENTIAL FOR THOSE WITH ANXIETY OR PANIC-RELATED SYMPTOMS TO OVERCOME THE ANXIOUS ISSUES!

Improving Sleep by Diaphragmatic Breathing and the Irony of a Restless Mind

Meditation- it allows the mind and body to rest by making a conscious effort of self-managing personal awareness of functioning.

People often misunderstand the concept of meditation and ascribe the picture of a monk or lotus position to meditating. For some, the result is that they do not further consider the benefits to meditation for their improved health. The central point that I have always attempted to make with individuals who claim that they can't sleep (usually point to a restless mind) is, **DON'T TRY TO STOP YOUR MIND FROM WORKING-JUST REDIRECT YOUR WORKING MIND TOWARDS ALLOWING YOU TO SLEEP RESTFULLY BY FOCUSING ON YOUR BREATHING.**

Let your mind work for you rather than against you. It is easy, and the key is to focus the restless mind towards the goal of self-awareness to achieve sleep. There is a simple way to accomplish this (I have utilized it for over 45 years and it works!) Here is how it works-

Meditating for Consistent Restful Sleep (Progressive Relaxation)

Step 1- get in a comfortable position so that you can fall off to sleep (or relax).

Step 2 – begin Diaphragmatic Breathing and concentrate the mind on the entire breathing process and the air going into the body (belly out-not chest), being expelled (belly in), and the restful feeling that comes over you. Once you have gotten into a rhythm-

Step 3 – Concentrate on each part of the body (in order) and concentrate on taking all tension and muscle tightness out of each area in turn. Meanwhile, continue concentration on your breathing (do not hyperventilate).

Step 4 – Concentrate on the fingers and toe (taking out the tension and relaxing them), then the hands and feet (same process), then the legs and arms (same process), then the trunk (belly and chest), then the neck and back, and lastly, the facial muscles and a total concentration on the body for relaxing totally.
Diaphragmatic Breathing-We Can Learn By Observing a Baby's Breathing

(WK-3)

STRESS-INNOCULATION CHECKLIST- A Self-Assessment Checklist

If it doesn't matter 5 years from now- don't worry about it	Does it matter?	Determine based on cost <u>vs</u> benefit OR pros <u>vs</u> cons
If it's a good idea now it will be a good idea next week	Is it an emergency or present-moment emergency?	Act if yes, Delay and Think about it further otherwise.
While reviewing day at its end- Are you happy with how you lived the day?	If no- If yes-	Don't worry about it, sleep, take care of it tomorrow. Don't worry, sleep instead.
Do you have your NEEDS met?	If yes- If no-	Don't stress over WANTS- they are not needs. Focus energies on actions rather than on worrying about it.
Do not expect others to live up to your expectations.	If you do- If you don't-	Are you responsible for them-take charge and give guidance. Otherwise-question self as to, why the expectations? Cost Benefit Or Pros /Cons problem-solving to determine relationship

(WK-4)

PURPOSE FOR MY LIFE EXERCISE-

What I Want to Be Known for Having Done When People Talk About my Life-

_____
_____
_____
_____.

Plan – I will achieve this Goal in Order for my Purpose to be Accomplished- Goal is _____ _____ _____ _____ _____.
I must complete these Steps for this Goal to be Reached- Goal Steps- a._____. Steps- b._____. Steps- c._____. Steps- d. _____. Steps- e._____. Steps- f. _____.
I must complete these Tasks for the Steps to be Completed- Task- 1. _____. Task- 2. _____. Task- 3. _____. Task- 4. _____. Task- 5. _____. Task- 6. _____. Task- 7. _____.
My estimated date for Completion is _____. This Goal is 1 of _____(how many total) to be completed in order to achieve my Plan. This Plan is 1 of _____(how many total) to be completed in order to achieve my Purpose in Life.

(WK 5)

The IDEAL Problem-Solving Method- A Checklist Approach

THE 5 STEPS TO THE PROCESS ARE:
Identify (Problem), Determine (Issues), Evaluate (Options/Solutions), Activate (Chosen Option), and Learn (From the Problem-Solving Process).

Step #1- Identifying the problem
This may be the hardest part of the process as there are times when what has happened previous to the event (earlier in the day, week, year, or even earlier) are the cause for our anger or stress.
There may be more than one problem to consider-if so, which one needs to be dealt with first, or, does the problem really even need to be directly addressed?
Will the problem lead to another situation if resolved? If so, what and is it better to table the issue until a more permanent solution can be devised to handle everything?
Is the problem yourself? Is it not a problem and only you are angry or negatively affected?

Step #2 – Determin(e)ing the issues
The easiest way to use this step is to ask yourself the question of "who, what, where, when, why, and how". If you can answer each of these parts to analyze and determine the problem, then you will tend to settle on understanding what specifically is at stake and where there are issues.

Another reasonable question to ask is "who are the stakeholders in the problem?" this is important to determine who has to be taken into account when a decision is reached. People matter and a prosocial approach to problem-solving requires all parties to be respected, secured, and considered.

Step #3- Evaluat(e)ing the options
Does the option resolve the problem totally or is something else (or additional steps) required to completely resolve all of the issues of the problem?
Ensure that no one is detrimentally affected by the options or choices you lean towards as a solution.
Is it efficient? You don't spend $10 dollars to handle a .05 (cent) problem.
What is the best option among those available?
Are you satisfied with the expected results or is more to be considered? (Go back to step 1 and go forward with each different issue as is appropriate and in a timely manner).

Step #4 – Act

Seemingly simple as a step, knowing when to act is just important as doing so in a productive, effective, and cost-conscious manner.

Sometimes it is best to allow someone the opportunity to correct the issues rather than always take charge-however, have an option available to use if it becomes important and necessary to act.

Don't hurt others unless it is not possible to avoid doing so-and-only if they are the proximal cause of the problem. Regardless, be considerate that they may be expected to tender the same regard for you in the future- "Don't cause yourself future problems" is a reasonable consideration.

Always have a plan in place to abort the actions if necessary.

Step #5 - Learn

An old adage is that there is never failure when one learns from a mistake. Keep this in mind and avoid thinking that once solved, it is the end of it. For everything that is resolved there is a follow-up (cause-and-effect in operation).

Military protocol is to have a "debriefing" after every exercise, action, or operation. Consider this process (learning) an opportunity to debrief yourself and those involved in the problem so that all can learn different, better, more effective, etc. ways to handle similar situations in the future.

Allow this process to give you confidence and elevate your self-esteem as you demonstrate competence in dealing with life. This is preferred to experiencing situations of anxiety, depression, mania, or dysfunctional personality related behaviors due to irrational thinking as has been described.

(WK 6)

THOUGHT BLOCKING EXERCISE- (Be creative and use those things that you like).

Ask yourself what things that you really like- hobbies, sports, music, etc. are examples of some things people like. PICK ONE, THEN,

Concentrate of what you picked, ASK YOURSELF, 5 questions to focus on about the thing that you picked.

WHAT is so good about it?

WHY do you like it?

How is it so good?

WHERE did you go to enjoy it?

HOW did you enjoy it?

WHEN did you enjoy it?

The idea is to fully understand the What, Why, How, Where, and When about your thing etc.

Spend time fully thinking with ALL of your concentration on answering these questions for yourself- then, Ask yourself-

AM I STILL THINKING ABOUT WHAT WAS BOTHERING ME?

IF STILL BOTHERED BY THE THOUGHTS-

  A. Count backwards by 7's from 1,000 (that takes full concentration), or,
  B. Count backwards from the end of the alphabet (letter 26) by 4's (every forth letter). That takes real concentration.

TRY TO DEVISE WAYS THAT WILL MAKE YOU FOCUS AND ADD CONCENTRATION BY ROUTINELY PRACTICING THESE THOUGHT BLOCKING TECHNIQUES.

(WK-7)
THOUGHT ATTACKING- Actively Questioning Accuracy of Thinking

Step 1-
Is The Thought True?

No-
Then Forget It,

Yes:
Ask yourself:
Is The Thought True without Any
Doubt At All?

No-
Then question why
you had the thought

Yes:
Ask yourself:
How does the Thought make you
feel (physically, emotionally,
stress, etc.)

Also Consider Stress   Inoculation
Plan (WK-3)

Physically panicky, worried, depressed,
or anxious:

Use Diaphragmic breathing/relaxation
strategy.

Mentally stressed:

Use Metacognitive Exercise
(WK 1)

Monitor the results of the various methods used in Step 3
Additional tools to use include Exercise or Thought Blocking (WK6)